3D Models in Motion
Using OpenGL

by D. James Benton

Preface

This is a second course on creating interactive models, building on my previous book, *3D Rendering in Windows*. In this text we will cover the finer details of code and object development. We will also explore how to implement advanced features and controls. The Windows® operating system and OpenGL® rendering engine will be our platform, but the same principles apply equally well to other environments. We will also proceed under the assumption that the reader is familiar with programming for the Windows® operating system and will not dwell on such details. Many references are available on that subject, including my book, *Version Independent Programming*. As in that text, we will require that <u>all</u> code function properly on <u>any</u> version and configuration of Windows®. All of the software described herein is available free online.

All of the examples contained in this book,
(as well as a lot of free programs) are available at...
https://www.dudleybenton.altervista.org/software/index.html

i

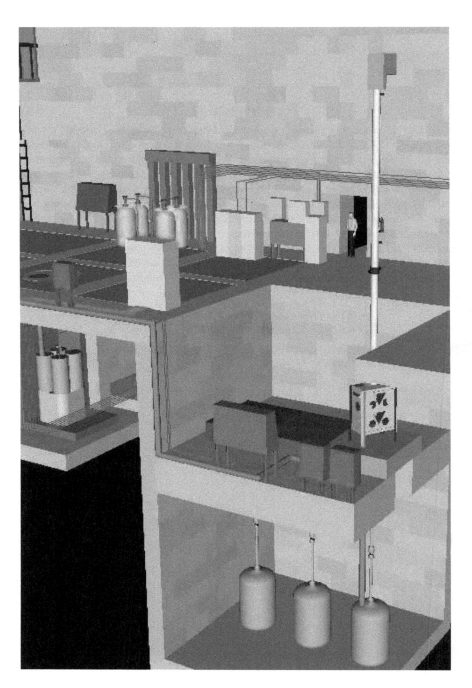

Table of Contents   page

Manhattan Project Virtual Museum

Chapter 1. Introduction

We will discuss some general aspects of 3D rendering, but our primary focus in this text will be implementation within the context of OpenGL® on the Windows® operating system. For additional details and more specifics, refer to my text, *3D Rendering in Windows*, available from Amazon:

https://www.amazon.com/dp/B01KG97XB8

There are four essential parts of an interactive 3D model are:

1) Graphical User Interface (GUI)
2) Pixel Rendering Context (PRC)
3) Three-Dimensional Objects (3DO)
4) Rendering Instruction Set (RIS)

We must also have the operating system (in this case Windows) and the rendering engine (in this case OpenGL). These combine to produce the final result—an interactive 3D model.

Graphical User Interface

This part of the whole is much like any other application. It performs the basic tasks of program loading, memory allocation, and file I/O.

Pixel Rendering Context

The OpenGL rendering engine requires a *pixel context* in order to deliver the result. An image is created within this context and then painted into a window that is a part of the GUI. The pixel context must have certain characteristics in order to implement the desired model building. See Appendix A for more on pixel contexts. Once the model is rendered into the pixel context, it can be displayed within the GUI.

3D Objects

Other than lines, all 3D objects are flat surfaces. There are no *solid* or *smooth* objects. All surfaces are composed of triangles or quadrangles. Even spheres, cylinders, and rolling hills are combinations of simpler polygons: triangles or quadrangles. While the rendering engine will accept a hexagon, this will ultimately be painted as six triangles.

All surfaces are either colored based on the vertices or draped with an image. A polygon may have a single color or this may vary linearly between the vertices using simple 2D interpolation for each of the color components. Draping images are called *textures* and have four components, abbreviated RGBA (red, green, blue, additional). The fourth parameter (given the symbol A) can be used in several ways to produce different visual effects. Windows 24 bit images are ordered BGR (blue, green, red) and must be reordered before passing them to the OpenGL rendering engine as a bound texture.

1

Rendering Instructions

The way OpenGL works is very simple (though not easy or trivial)... You first clear the pixel context, set up the lighting, and define the viewpoint (which might be thought of as the camera position). You then send all of the 3D objects to the rendering engine. After this is complete, you paint the result onto a window within the GUI. While you can change some things inside the pixel context after building it and also add more items, the normal procedure is to clear and then rebuild everything. This process eliminates ambiguities and also determines the rate of animation, which is limited by the time required to clear and rebuild.

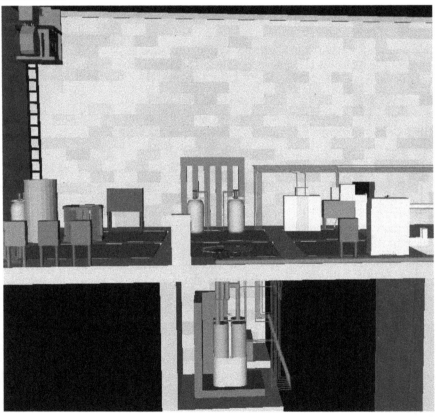

Chapter 2. Geometric Shapes

All of the geometric shapes are illustrated in the Demo3D example, which can be found in the online archive in folder examples\Demo3D. We first build a small function to receive a polygon and pass this along to the rendering engine. The polygons should be convex and non-overlapping. Concave and/or overlapping polygons should be first subdivided into triangles and combined to form a *mesh*, which we will discuss in the next chapter. All simple geometric shapes can be built up from polygons. For instance, a cylinder is formed entirely from quadrangles:

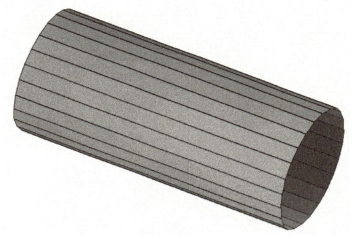

Spheroids are formed of quadrangles plus triangles at the poles.

A torus is formed entirely of quadrangles.

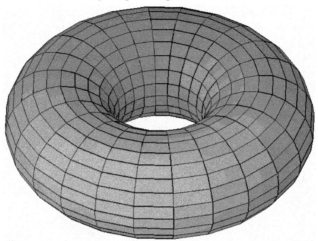

A cone is formed from triangles and a disc (i.e., a washer) is formed from quadrangles. More elaborate shapes such as a spring are easily formed from these basic polygons.

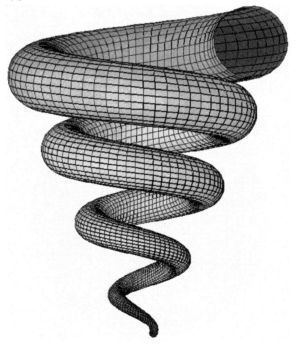

Many simple shapes can be created by extruding quadrangles along a curve.

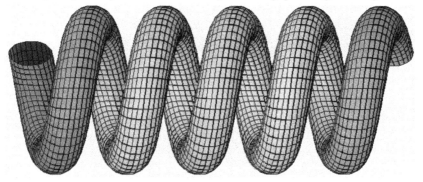

Simple distortions can also be applied.

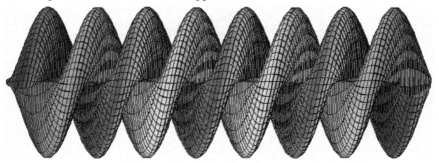

Distortions, stretching, and twists can be combined.

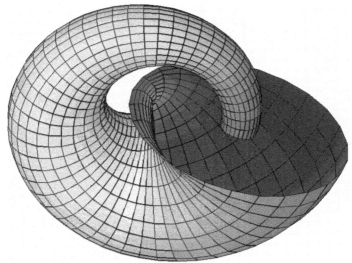

The entire range of polyhedra can be quickly assembled from a few polygons. Walls are easily formed using hexahedra (i.e., bricks).

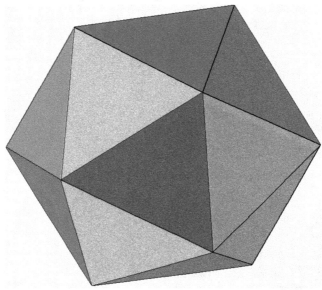

The following simple functions can be used to pass each of these shapes and more to the rendering engine.

```
void RenderTriangle(VECTOR V1,VECTOR V2,VECTOR V3,COLOR
  c)
  {
  VECTOR N;
  glBegin(GL_TRIANGLES);
  glMaterialfv(glFace(),GL_AMBIENT_AND_DIFFUSE,c);
  N=vNormal(V1,V2,V3);
  glNormal3d(N.x,N.y,N.z);
  glVertex3d(V1.x,V1.y,V1.z);
  glVertex3d(V2.x,V2.y,V2.z);
  glVertex3d(V3.x,V3.y,V3.z);
  glEnd();
  }
void RenderQuadrangle(VECTOR V1,VECTOR V2,VECTOR
  V3,VECTOR V4,COLOR c)
  {
  VECTOR N;
  glBegin(GL_QUADS);
  glMaterialfv(glFace(),GL_AMBIENT_AND_DIFFUSE,c);
  N=vNormal(V1,V2,V3);
  glNormal3d(N.x,N.y,N.z);
  glVertex3d(V1.x,V1.y,V1.z);
```

6

```
glVertex3d(V2.x,V2.y,V2.z);
glVertex3d(V3.x,V3.y,V3.z);
glVertex3d(V4.x,V4.y,V4.z);
glEnd();
}
```

Along with defining the coordinates of the vertices and color, we must also define the outward normal so that the rendering engine can properly apply lighting. The outward normal vector is the cross product of the two vectors forming the vertices of the triangle.

```
VECTOR vNormal(VECTOR V1,VECTOR V2,VECTOR V3)
{
double a1,a2,a3,b1,b2,b3,r;
static VECTOR N;
a1=V2.x-V1.x;
a2=V2.y-V1.y;
a3=V2.z-V1.z;
b1=V3.x-V1.x;
b2=V3.y-V1.y;
b3=V3.z-V1.z;
N.x=a2*b3-a3*b2;
N.y=a3*b1-a1*b3;
N.z=a1*b2-a2*b1;
r=sqrt(N.x*N.x+N.y*N.y+N.z*N.z);
if(r>DBL_EPSILON)
    {
    N.x/=r;
    N.y/=r;
    N.z/=r;
    }
else
    {
    N.x=0;
    N.y=0;
    N.z=1;
    }
return(N);
}
```

Chapter 3. Meshes

A mesh is an unstructured assemblage of polygons, most often triangles or quadrangles. It's basically the same as a finite element grid and programs designed to generate such grids can be used to create and manipulate these 3D objects. This surface was created from triangles.

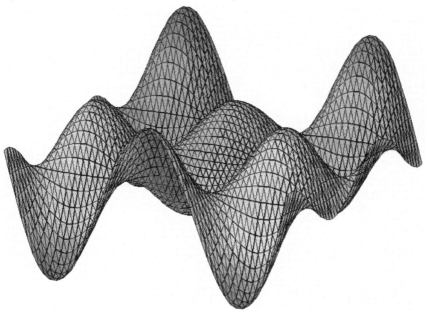

This is a more complex mesh, fitted to the topography:

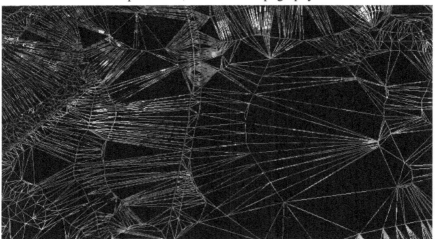

Several mesh-generating tools are available on the web. There is a free tool with source code (elem3.c) on my web site listed in the Forward. You will find it in the archive accompanying the text, *Differential Equations*. It was used to produce the following mesh.

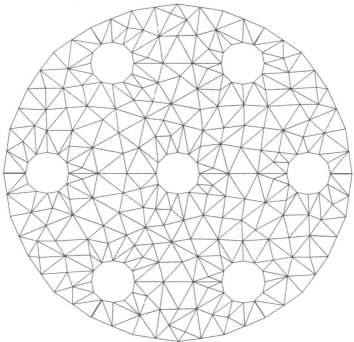

and also this 3D rendering:

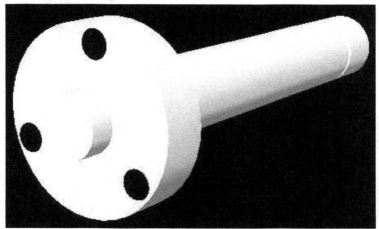

It is most efficient to define and deliver polygons in a mesh structure, each polygon having an assigned color or texture. As the three components of RGB only occupy the lower 24 of 32 bits in a standard unsigned integer, any value in the high byte (-1, which is 0xFFFFFFFF) can be used to terminate a list.

```
MESH mesh[]={
    {1,2,3,4,5,6,7,8,9,blue},
    {2,3,4,5,6,7,8,9,1,red},
    {3,4,5,6,7,8,9,1,2,green},
    {0,0,0,0,0,0,0,0,0,-1}};
```

The most famous model associated with OpenGL is the teapot, as the developers used this object to test their work along the way. This teapot is a distorted ellipsoid plus two warped curving tubes.

The ellipsoid is composed of quadrangles with triangles at the poles and the tubes are entirely quadrangles.

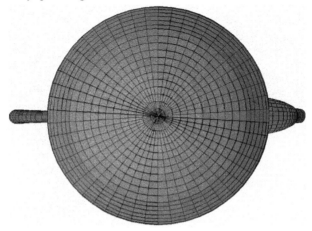

OpenGL provides smooth shading.

A Klein bottle can be formed entirely from quadrangles.

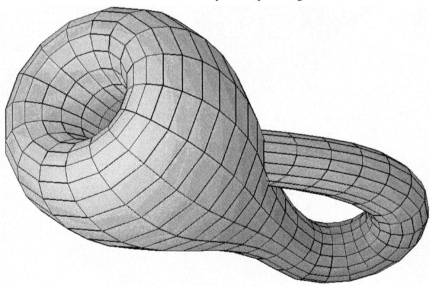

For more on meshes, see Appendix E.

Chapter 4. Complex Objects

Complex objects are most easily constructed as a mesh or collection of meshes. The board and chess pieces are mesh objects.

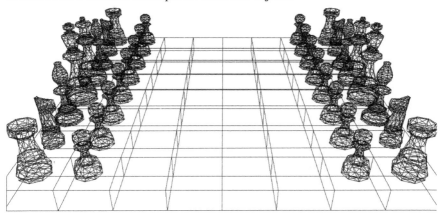

The final result after painting is shown below.

Each piece is a mesh at the origin (x=y=z=0), as shown below:

```
PIECE bishop[]={
{-1652,    -7,    0,-1168,    -7, 1168,-1504,    66,     0},
{-1652,    -7,    0,-1504,    66,     0,-1064,    66,-1064},
{-1652,    -7,    0,-1064,    66,-1064,-1168,     -7,-1168},
{-1652,    -7,    0,-1168,    -7,-1168, -884,     9,     0},
{-1652,    -7,    0, -884,     9,     0, -625,     9,   625},
{-1652,    -7,    0, -625,     9,   625,-1168,    -7, 1168},
{-1644,   413,    0,-1163,   413, 1163,-1409,   717,     0},
{-1644,   413,    0,-1409,   717,     0, -996,   717, -996},
{-1644,   413,    0, -996,   717, -996,-1163,   413,-1163},
```

These are then drawn at the desired location and rotation by a small section of code:

```
void RenderPiece(MESH*piece,char*object,DWORD
    texture,float x,float z,float s,float b)
  {
  int k;
  k=ObjectIndex(object);
  glPushMatrix();
  glTranslatef(x,0,z);
  glScalef(s,s,s);
  glStencilFunc(GL_ALWAYS,k,-1);
  glRotatef(b,0,1,0);
  if(k==selected)
    glMesh(piece,0xFF0000,0);
  else
    glMesh(piece,0,texture);
  glStencilFunc(GL_ALWAYS,0,-1);
  glPopMatrix();
  }
```

The board is a collection of hexahedra (bricks):

```
void RenderBoard()
  {
  char board[]="??";
  int i,j,k;
  for(i=0;i<8;i++)
    {
    board[1]='1'+i;
    for(j=0;j<8;j++)
      {
      board[0]='A'+j;
      k=ObjectIndex(board);
      glStencilFunc(GL_ALWAYS,k,-1);
      if(k==selected)
        glHexahedron(Brd[i],-3./32.,Brd[j],
          3./8.,3./16.,3./8.,0xFF0000,0);
      else
        glHexahedron(Brd[i],-3./32.,Brd[j],
          3./8.,3./16.,3./8.,0,
          (i+j)%2?light_stone:dark_stone);
      }
    }
  glStencilFunc(GL_ALWAYS,0,-1);
  }
```

Three-dimensional models for all sorts of things (e.g., man, fire extinguisher, and forklift palette) are available online and can be readily adapted to the mesh structure best suited to construct your ensemble within the OpenGL context, as illustrated by this next figure:

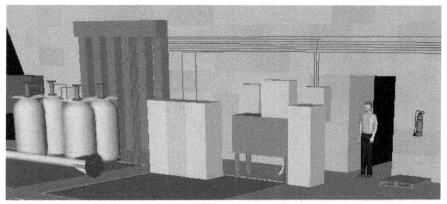

Other objects (e.g., tanks, cabinets, and panels) can be created with geometric shapes, such as the iconic (and unusually-shaped) water tower associated with the East Tennessee Technology Park since the Manhattan Project.

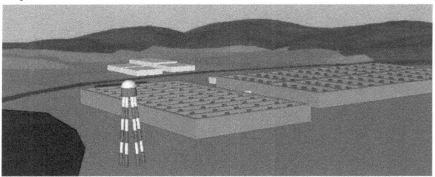

As illustrated with the chess pieces, many objects can be quickly rendered bi the OpenGL engine so that even complex assemblies, such as the following section, can be created. This assembly consists of six ribbed tanks, twelve centrifugal compressors, twelve electric motors with shaft, housing, and mounting block, twenty pipes, walls, and slab.

```
MESH Motor0[]={
   { 0.762F, 0.000F, 0.429F, 0.660F, 0.381F, 0.429F,
     0.667F, 0.000F, 0.594F,0.F,0.F,0.F,dodger_blue},
   { 0.577F, 0.333F, 0.594F, 0.667F, 0.000F, 0.594F,
     0.660F, 0.381F, 0.429F,0.F,0.F,0.F,dodger_blue},
   { 0.667F, 0.000F, 0.594F, 0.577F, 0.333F, 0.594F,
     0.476F, 0.000F, 0.594F,0.F,0.F,0.F,dodger_blue},
   { 0.412F, 0.238F, 0.594F, 0.476F, 0.000F, 0.594F,
     0.577F, 0.333F, 0.594F,0.F,0.F,0.F,dodger_blue},
   etc...
```

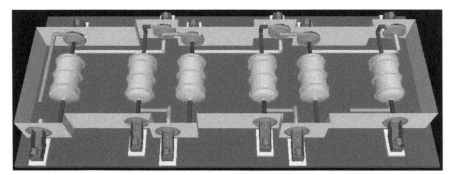

Any level of complexity can be assembled in this way.

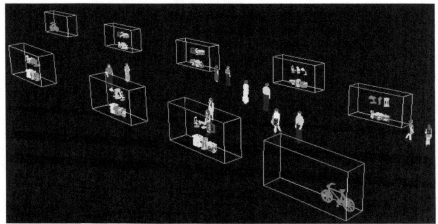

For more on complex objects, see Appendix E.

Chapter 5. Textured Objects

Except for the chess pieces, all of the objects presented thus far have been simply colored. Textures are an important aspect of OpenGL that provides realism. Textures are bitmaps (i.e., flat colored images) that are draped over the polygons. These must be properly prepared before they can be used. Texture preparation involves four steps:

1) Load into memory

2) Convert to correct format

3) Associate with an index

4) Bind to the vertices

The image format expected by OpenGL is unlike Windows or JPEG, as development of OpenGL predates the widespread availability of both Windows and JPEG (see Appendix B for more details). Images can be loaded in several ways, including:

1) Data statement (very large)

2) Resource

3) File

A simple program can be written to convert any binary file (such as a JPEG) to a data statement. Resources are specified in a RC file, processed by the resource compiler, and linked with the program. These must then be loaded into active memory (see Appendix C for more details). Once converted to the proper format (see Appendix B for details), an index must be issued by the rendering engine through a call to glGenTextures(). You will always refer to this texture by the assigned index. After receiving the index, the image is associated with it through a call to glBindTexture().

Textures (i.e., bitmap images) are two-dimensional (i.e., flat). You must define 2D single precision floating point coordinates of the texture (zero to one) with the 3D vertices of your objects as you pass each point to the rendering engine. The simplest sequence is illustrated in the following code snippet that paints a picture onto a rectangle (hence 0,0 to 1,0 to 1,1 to 0,1):

```
loop through polygons
  {
  BindTexture(GL_TEXTURE_2D,texture_index);
  glEnable(GL_TEXTURE_2D);
  glColor(white);
  glBegin(GL_QUADS);
  glNormal3f(0,0,1);
  glTexCoord2d(0,0);glVertex3f(x-w/2,z-h/2,y);
  glTexCoord2d(1,0);glVertex3f(x+w/2,z-h/2,y);
  glTexCoord2d(1,1);glVertex3f(x+w/2,z+h/2,y);
  glTexCoord2d(0,1);glVertex3f(x-w/2,z+h/2,y);
  glEnd();
```

```
glDisable(GL_TEXTURE_2D);
}
```

First bind the texture using the index provided. Enable textures. Use white light. Begin a sequence of (in this case one) quadrangle. Specify the outward normal vector. Specify four texture coordinates and four polygon points sequentially. End the quadrangle sequence. Disable textures before you paint anything else. Draping textures over more complex options requires some creative mathematics, as illustrated in the chess program, which may be found in the online archive in folder examples\chess.

Not only are textures rectangular, both dimensions (height and width) must be a power of two. This makes draping textures over some shapes challenging. Several illustrations of texture draping can be found in the codes contained in the online archive in the examples folder.

One such transformation is spherical, as illustrated in this next figure:

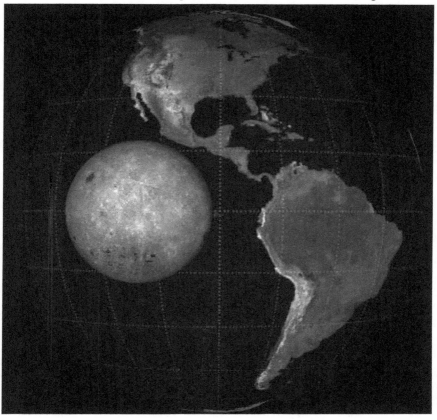

The original flat undistorted image used for these textures is rectangular:

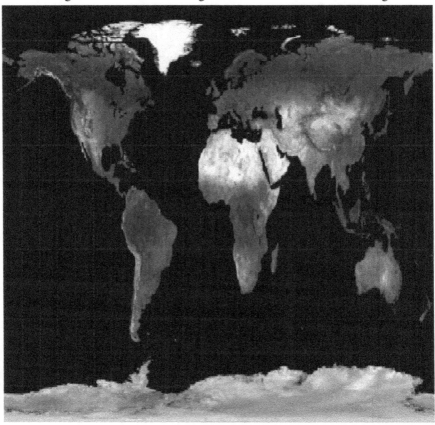

The texture coordinates are (0,0) in the bottom left corner and (1,1) in the upper right. In order to wrap this around a sphere (coordinates r,θ,φ), we apply the relationships:

$$x = \frac{1+\cos(\theta)}{2}$$
$$y = \frac{1+\cos(\varphi)}{2}$$

(5.1)

Chapter 6. Viewpoint

The OpenGL rendering engine works with a view port (a frame containing a distorted but flat picture of the objects) and a camera (the eye of the observer).

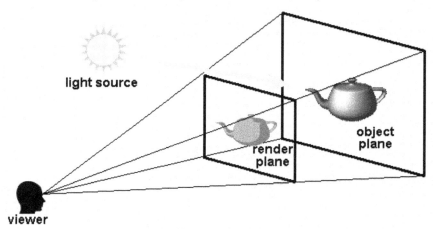

Setting the view port is simple and must be adjusted whenever the target window is changed inside the GUI with a call to the engine:

```
SetViewport(width,height);
```

The camera is a little more complicated, having three angles (roll, pitch, and yaw) and three translations (heave, sway, and surge), best described by the motions of a ship.

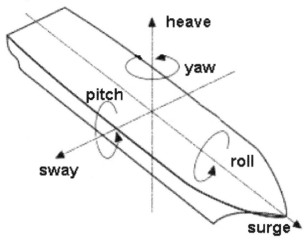

The OpenGL axis orientation began from 2D representations, as this came to computers first. The X-axis is from left to right. The Y-axis is from bottom to top (on a flat display). The Z-axis then arises from the cross product of X and Y, which is positive out of the display toward the viewer and negative into the display away from the viewer.

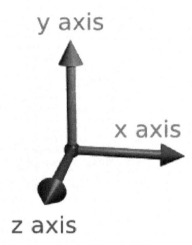

Thus, surge is in the positive X direction, heave is in the positive Y direction and sway is in the positive Z direction. The rotations are defined by the right-hand thumb rule from the three axis directions, as indicated on the ship. After setting the view port and before drawing the objects, we set the six camera variables by three rotations (which must be must be performed in three steps in order to work as expected by the typical observer), three translations (which can be performed in a single step), and an optional scaling (stretching or shrinking in all three dimensions). The scaling can be done before or after the translation, though the effect is different. This is illustrated by the following code snippet:

```
glRotatef((float)view.a,1.F,0.F,0.F);
glRotatef((float)view.b,0.F,1.F,0.F);
glRotatef((float)view.c,0.F,0.F,1.F);
glScalef(view.s,view.s,view.s);
glTranslatef(view.x,view.y,view.z);
```

For example, when the user clicks on a button, moves a slider, or depresses a key, the scene is cleared, the updated camera variables are sent to the rendering engine, followed by the objects, and the result is painted back into the space provided by the GUI. In this way the user can rotate, translate, and zoom the scene.

Chapter 7. Lighting

We will not discuss complex lighting in this text. The reader is directed to my previous text, *3D Rendering in Windows*, and many other articles on the subject. Our focus here is on 3D models that do something in response to user inputs, for example, illustrate procedures for training. The reactor simulator provided as an example throughout this text was used for this very purpose. Maximal realism in rendering might be desirable for some applications. Here we are concerned with function over form—how it works more so than how it looks. While more than one light is available (limited to two on some systems), we will use only one simple white light (index zero), whose position is defined in spherical coordinates and is sufficiently distant from the objects as to be essentially infinite. This is accomplished with a few calls to the OpenGL rendering engine:

```
glLightModeli(GL_LIGHT_MODEL_TWO_SIDE,FALSE);
glLightModeli(GL_LIGHT_MODEL_LOCAL_VIEWER,FALSE);
glLightModelfv(GL_LIGHT_MODEL_AMBIENT,
  floatColor(0x000000));
glLightfv(GL_LIGHT0,GL_AMBIENT ,floatColor(0x777777));
glLightfv(GL_LIGHT0,GL_DIFFUSE ,floatColor(0x999999));
glLightfv(GL_LIGHT0,GL_SPECULAR,floatColor(0x000000));
lp[0]=sin(Light.a*M_PI/180)*cos(Light.b*M_PI/180);
lp[2]=cos(Light.a*M_PI/180)*cos(Light.b*M_PI/180);
lp[1]=sin(Light.b*M_PI/180);
lp[3]=0;/* infinite distance to light source */
glLightfv(GL_LIGHT0,GL_POSITION,lp);
glEnable(GL_LIGHT0);
glEnable(GL_LIGHTING);
```

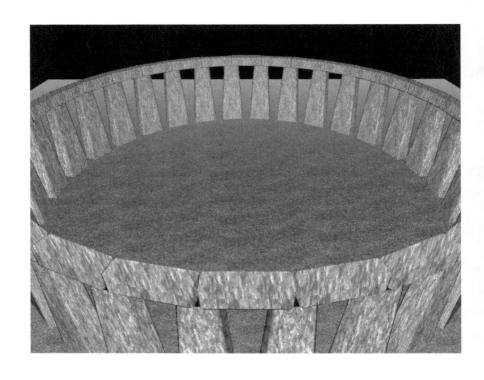

Chapter 8. Simple Motion

An example of simple motion would be rotating the view through 360° in steps of 15° about the Y-axis (red vector). The following code (which can be found in the SWSA5 example in the online archive) accomplishes this. The steps (clear, rebuild, paint) are all performed in user-defined function RePaint().

```
if(msg.message==WM_COMMAND&&msg.wParam==PUSH_ROTATE)
  {
  int b;
  for(b=0;b<360;b+=15)
    {
    view.b=b;
    RePaint();
    }
  SetFocus(hMain);
  return(TRUE);
  }
```

After pushing a button or clicking on some object, it is necessary to return focus to the main program using SetFocus(hMain); otherwise, the 3D keystrokes will not be directed to the correct message stream. This is an important detail of Windows GUI programming. The end result is something like the following:

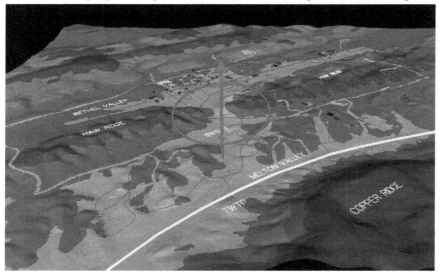

Rotation about the X-axis is accomplished using view.a and about the Z-axis using view.c then repainting. This moves the object via changing the view structure:

```
struct{int a,b,c,h,w;float s,x,y,z;}view;
```

25

If, instead, we wanted to follow along Melton Valley, as indicated by the orange curve in the preceding figure, we would move the camera, not the object, by changing the camera structure:

```
struct{float a,b,c;}camera;
```

We step the camera along the X-axis (camera.a) and the Z-axis (camera.c), repainting at each step, following the arc indicated by the thick yellow curve. The scene has been conveniently scaled to fit into a zero to one frame. The applicable code is:

```
if(msg.message==WM_COMMAND&&msg.wParam==PUSH_PATH)
  {
  float path[]={
    {0.24F,0.00F},
    {0.28F,0.05F},
    {0.32F,0.09F},
    {0.35F,0.13F},
    {0.39F,0.17F},
    {0.43F,0.20F},
    {0.47F,0.24F},
    {0.51F,0.27F},
    {0.54F,0.30F},
    {0.58F,0.33F},
    {0.62F,0.36F},
    {0.66F,0.38F},
    {0.70F,0.40F},
    {0.73F,0.42F},
    {0.77F,0.44F},
    {0.81F,0.46F},
    {0.85F,0.48F},
    {0.89F,0.49F},
    {0.92F,0.50F},
    {0.96F,0.51F},
    {1.00F,0.52F},
    {FLT_MAX}};
  for(i=0;path[i]!=FLT_MAX;i++)
    {
    camera.a-=path[i++];
    camera.c+=path[i];
    RePaint();
    }
  SetFocus(hMain);
  return(TRUE);
  }
```

Note that floating point numbers are double precision by default; whereas, OpenGL expects single precision floats. The compiler will issue a warning if the data statements do not include the designation F. Several of the examples include a "tour" button that implements just such a stepping process. While the camera and view structures could be combined, I prefer to keep them separate so that it is clear in the code which one is being modified.

Moving Objects within a Scene

These examples have considered fixed objects within a scene, moving the entire scene or moving the camera with respect to the scene. We might want to move some objects within a scene. Perhaps the simplest of these is the Earth and Moon demo, where the Earth rotates and the Moon orbits. This implementation is not astronomically correct, as this would be quite boring and slow indeed. It takes 29 days, 12 hours, 44 minutes, and 3 seconds for the Moon to orbit the Earth. In this demo it's only 8 days (see turn/8 below). The moon also rotates so that the same side is always facing the Earth. This would require an additional step, not included in the following simple code. The loosely implemented orbiting requires two steps, the first being:

```
if(msg.message=WM_COMMAND&&msg.wParam==PUSH_ROTATE)
  {
  int t;
  for(t=120;t>0;t--)
  {
  turn=t;
  RePaint();
  }
  SetFocus(hMain);
  return(TRUE);
  }
```

and the second being:

```
void RePaint(void)
  {
/* set lighting */
  glClear(GL_COLOR_BUFFER_BIT|GL_DEPTH_BUFFER_BIT);
  glLightfv(GL_LIGHT0,GL_POSITION,LightPos);
  glEnable(GL_TEXTURE_2D);
  glLightfv(GL_LIGHT0,GL_DIFFUSE,White);
  glLightfv(GL_LIGHT0,GL_SPECULAR,Black);
/* rotate view */
  glPushMatrix();
  glRotatef(90.,1.,0.,0.);
/* draw Earth */
  glPushMatrix();
  glRotatef(turn,0.,0.,1.);
  glTexImage2D(GL_TEXTURE_2D,0,3,nEarth,nEarth,
    0,GL_RGB,GL_UNSIGNED_BYTE,tEarth);
  glCallList(gEarth);
  glPopMatrix();
/* draw Moon */
  glTexImage2D(GL_TEXTURE_2D,0,3,nMoon,nMoon,
    0,GL_RGB,GL_UNSIGNED_BYTE,tMoon);
```

```
glRotatef(turn/8.,0.,0.,1.);
glTranslatef(0.,3.,0.);
glCallList(gMoon);
glPopMatrix();
glutSwapBuffers();
}
```

We note several things here. First, the steps: clear, lighting, rotate, render Earth, render Moon, swap buffers. The last step paints the rendered result into the window provided by the GUI. Function glRotatef() is called performed before rendering the Earth and Moon plus glTranslatef() is called before rendering the Moon. This puts the two objects in the correct place. Each texture is selected just before rendering the sphere by calling glTexImage2D().

While we could draw the two spheres (Earth and Moon) by feeding triangles around each pole and quadrangles over the rest of the surface. We use a convenient feature of OpenGL: lists. Using lists may not make rendering any faster, but it does simplify parts of the code making the overall flow more clear. A sphere is a special type of set recognized by OpenGL and so defining a list that happens to be a sphere is a simple process (see Appendix D for more on working with lists).

```
Quadric=gluNewQuadric();
gluQuadricTexture(Quadric,GL_TRUE);
gEarth=glGenLists(1);
glNewList(gEarth,GL_COMPILE);
gluSphere(Quadric,2.,24,24);
glEndList();
```

This type of object is called a *quadric*, we want it to include a texture (bitmap), we must be assigned an integer by calling glGenLists(), we add one sphere, and then close out the list. We can now refer to the list by the index: gEarth. The same is done to create gMoon.

Chapter 9. Linkage Motion

We have already seen this simple type of motion in several examples, including: bluepony, gears, geartrain, origami, and rollercoaster. This is the technique used in the MSRE demo. We will begin with bluepony. The outer loop moves the whole pony around the OpenGL sign, much like the Moon orbiting the Earth. This is accomplished by the following code snippet:

```
xPos=WalkRadius*cos(WalkAngle*M_PI/180);
zPos=WalkRadius*sin(WalkAngle*M_PI/180);
glEnable(GL_LIGHTING);
glPushMatrix();
glTranslatef(xPos,0,zPos);
glRotatef(90-WalkAngle,0,1,0);
DrawPony(LegAngle);
glPopMatrix();
```

The sin() and cos() provide the orbiting location in the XZ plane. The pony is rotated along the orbit (variable WalkAngle) with a call to glRotatef(), which comes *after* the call to glTranslatef(). The pony is perpendicular to the radius (variable WalkRadius) by setting the rotation angle to 90-WalkAangle. Notice the call to glPushMatrix() and later glPopMatrix(). These save the transformation, which is changed during the pony drawing. The variable LegAngle is passed to the function rendering the pony, which we examine next...

```
void DrawPony(float legAngle)
  {
  glCallList(Body);
  glCallList(Mane);
  glPushMatrix();
  glTranslatef(FrontLegPos[0],FrontLegPos[1],
    FrontLegPos[2]);
  glRotatef(legAngle,0.0,0.0,1.0);
  glCallList(FrontLeg);
  glPopMatrix();
  glPushMatrix();
  glTranslatef(FrontLegPos[0],FrontLegPos[1],-
    FrontLegPos[2]);
  glRotatef(-legAngle,0.0,0.0,1.0);
  glCallList(FrontLeg);
  glPopMatrix();
  glPushMatrix();
  glTranslatef(BackLegPos[0],BackLegPos[1],
    BackLegPos[2]);
  glRotatef(-legAngle,0.0,0.0,1.0);
  glCallList(BackLeg);
  glPopMatrix();
  glPushMatrix();
```

```
glTranslatef(BackLegPos[0],BackLegPos[1],-
    BackLegPos[2]);
glRotatef(legAngle,0.0,0.0,1.0);
glCallList(BackLeg);
glPopMatrix();
}
```

Note the convenient use of lists to draw the parts of the pony. Notice also the section of code surrounding each part that is altered to produce the leg motion. This particular procedure has five steps:

1) Push the transformation matrix onto the stack
2) Apply the translation (x, y, z sliding)
3) Apply the rotation (α, θ, φ turning)
4) Render list
5) Pop the transformation off the stack

The two gear examples (gears.c and geartrain.c) are even simpler. Both were written by Brian Paul (author of bluepony) and adapted by Mark J. Kilgard, author of the GLUT OpenGL Utility Library. Here we see geartrain:

Gears (or similar objects) of the same shape, even of different sizes, can be defined by a single section of code, as the diameter, depth, tooth pitch, and number of teeth can be specified in an argument. These can be built beforehand

and kept in lists or generated each time. There are three distinct gear shapes in this example. We don't need to worry about meshing of the teeth, provided they are properly shaped, translated to the correct location, and set to the appropriate rotation before rendering. There is only one type of shaft, drawn four times. There is also only one belt. Rendering the scene can be facilitated with a few arrays so as to use three outer loops:

```
for(k=0;k<number_of_axles;k++)
  {
  for(i=0;i<number_of_gears-1;i++)
    {
    for(j=0;j<number_of_gears;j++)
```

The primary gear position is set and the others are calculated from it. One section of code illustrates how the gears are properly synchronized:

```
for(i=0;i<number_of_gears;i++)
  {
  x=y=z=0.;
  axle_index=axle_find(g[i].axle_name);
  g[i].axis=a[axle_index].axis;
  g[i].motored=a[axle_index].motored;
  if(a[axle_index].motored)
    {
    g[i].direction=a[axle_index].direction;

  g[i].angular_velocity=a[axle_index].angular_velocity;
    }
  if(g[i].axis==0)
    x=1.0;
  else if(g[i].axis==1)
    y=1.0;
  else
    z=1.0;
  g[i].position[0]=a[axle_index].position[0]
    +x*g[i].relative_position;
  g[i].position[1]=a[axle_index].position[1]
    +y*g[i].relative_position;
  g[i].position[2]=a[axle_index].position[2]
    +z*g[i].relative_position;
  }
```

Combined rotation and translation of the shaft in the MSRE demo is accomplished with only a few lines of code:

```
for(a=90;a>=0;a-=15)
  {
  PosiObject(crane,Vector(60.1-r*sin(a*M_PI/180),
    2.+r*cos(a*M_PI/180),27.4F),FALSE);
  PosiObject(probe_angle,Vector(0.F,0.F,a),TRUE);
  }
```

31

Dynamic repositioning of single and multiple (combined) objects is accomplished with only a few lines of code:

```
struct{int cols,rows,step;float*data,*high,*lift;
  }Animate;
void PosiObject(int object,VECTOR v,int next_step)
  {
  int j=Animate.cols*Animate.step+3*object;
  Animate.data[j+1]=v.x;
  Animate.data[j+2]=v.y+Animate.lift[object];
  Animate.data[j+3]=v.z;
  if(next_step)
    NextStep();
  }
void PosiObjects(float x,float z,int object,...)
  {
  int j;
  va_list arg_marker;
  va_start(arg_marker,object);
  while(object>=0)
    {
    j=Animate.cols*Animate.step+3*object;
    Animate.data[j+1]=x;
    Animate.data[j+3]=z;
    object=(int)va_arg(arg_marker,int);
    }
  NextStep();
  }
```

Steps along the process are stacked in a growing pile, which is reallocated as needed:

```
void NextStep()
  {
  int j;
  if(++Animate.step>=Animate.rows)
    {
    Animate.rows+=100;
    Animate.data=reallocate(__LINE__,Animate.data,
      Animate.cols*Animate.step,Animate.cols*
      Animate.rows,sizeof(float));
    }
  for(j=1;j<Animate.cols;j++)
    Animate.data[Animate.cols* Animate.step   +j]=
    Animate.data[Animate.cols*(Animate.step-1)+j];
  }
```

Note that there are two allocation functions in Windows: malloc() and calloc(). The first does not clear the memory, while the second does. There was a reallocate function in DOS, but this was not carried over to Windows. You must provide your own. Reallocation (expansion or contraction of an existing block of memory) involves three steps:

```
1) Allocate a new block
2) Copy the old block into the new
3) Free the old block
```

This is accomplished by the following code:

```
void*reallocate(int line,void*old_ptr,unsigned
   old_count,unsigned new_count,unsigned size)
 {
 void*new_ptr;
 if((new_ptr=calloc(new_count,size))==NULL)
   Abort(line,"can't reallocate memory %ux%u=%u "
     "-> %ux%u=%u bytes",old_count,size,old_count*
     size,new_count,size,new_count*size);
 if(old_ptr&&old_count)
   {
   memcpy(new_ptr,old_ptr,min(old_count,new_count)
     *size);
   free(old_ptr);
   }
 return(new_ptr);
 }
```

It is important to check for failure to allocate memory blocks, as such will result in a fatal exception and a program crash. While there may be plenty of available memory, allocation is not always successful and it is good practice to check. Checking also aids in troubleshooting.

The next linkage motion we will consider is the miniature steam engine example created by Troy Robinette using Mark Kilgard's OpenGL Utility Toolkit, GLUT. This model includes a crankshaft, flywheel, connecting rod, piston, cylinder, and pivot pin. The wire frame is shown on the next page. The motions are familiar. The piston slides up and down in the cylinder. In this case, rather than accentuating a wristpin, the rod and piston are rigid and the cylinder rocks back-and-forth to maintain alignment.

The position of each object is related by trigonometric relationships. The crankshaft and flywheel simply rotate. The rod boss follows the crank pin. The angle of the cylinder, piston, and rod are given by the Pythagorean theorem. The position of each part is determined from the crank angle, which is advanced to produce the animated effect.

The rendering sequence is as before: clear, set view and camera, render objects, and finally paint. This last step is accomplished by a call to the GLUT function glutPostRedisplay(). The lighting is unremarkable. An optional checkerboard texture is included for illustration and variety. Lists are used for each of the objects, which makes the code (steam.c) more readable. Use of the GLUT library eliminates the need for a specific GUI.

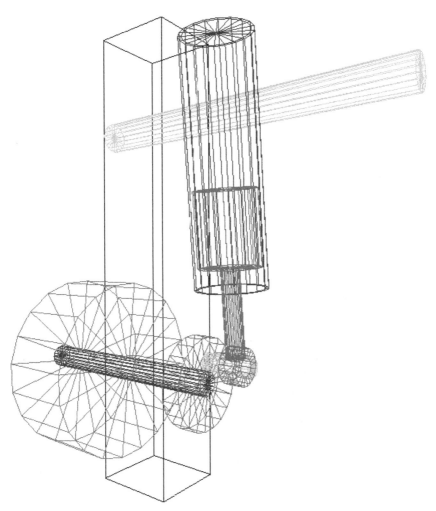

In order to reinforce the step-by-step approach of such models, we will consider just a few drawing procedures, beginning with the cylinder:

```
void draw_cylinder(GLUquadricObj*object,GLdouble
    outerRadius,GLdouble innerRadius,GLdouble lenght)
{
glPushMatrix();
gluCylinder(object,outerRadius,outerRadius,
    lenght,20,1);
glPushMatrix();
glRotatef(180,0.0,1.0,0.0);
gluDisk(object,innerRadius,outerRadius,20,1);
```

```
glPopMatrix();
glTranslatef(0.0,0.0,lenght);
gluDisk(object,innerRadius,outerRadius,20,1);
glPopMatrix();
}
```

Notice the call to glPushMatrix() at the beginning and glPopMatrix() at the end. This preserves orientation of the scene and other objects. Only this object is impacted by the call to glRotatef() and glTranslatef(). The piston is quite similar:

```
void draw_piston(void)
{
glPushMatrix();
glColor4f(0.3,0.6,0.9,1.0);
glPushMatrix();
glRotatef(90,0.0,1.0,0.0);
glTranslatef(0.0,0.0,-0.07);
myCylinder(obj,0.125,0.06,0.12);
glPopMatrix();
glRotatef(-90,1.0,0.0,0.0);
glTranslatef(0.0,0.0,0.05);
myCylinder(obj,0.06,0.0,0.6);
glTranslatef(0.0,0.0,0.6);
myCylinder(obj,0.2,0.0,0.5);
glPopMatrix();
}
```

There is an outer loop to rotate the assembly and the option for clockwise or counterclockwise. Because this example doesn't need much in the way of user interface code, it is a clear and concise example of programmed linkage motion.

```
do
  {
  draw_engine_pole();
  glPushMatrix();
  glTranslatef(0.5,1.4,0.0);
  draw_cylinder_head();
  glPopMatrix();
  glPushMatrix();
  glTranslatef(0.0,-0.8,0.0);
  draw_crank();
  glPopMatrix();
  }
while(pass>0);
```

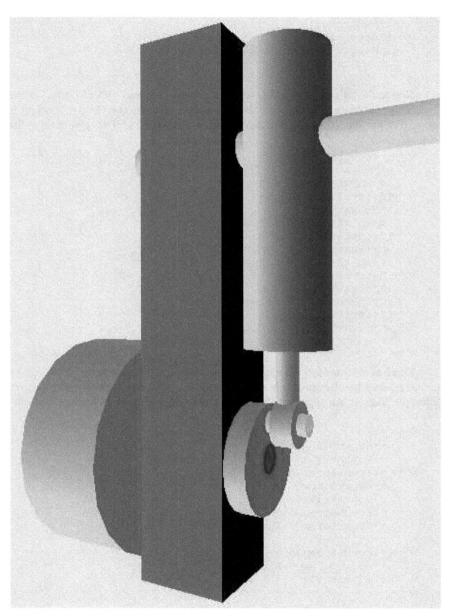

Linkage motion us used throughout the MSRE example, which may be found in the online archive. The MSRE scene is depicted on the cover. The cask is run through its paces using linkage motion, as shown in these next figures:

36

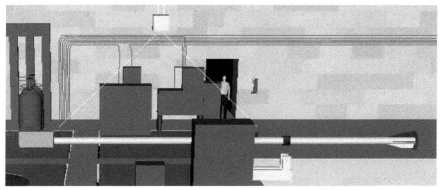

Each of the three dimensional components of the motion is interpolated (as a table) from the initial time to the final time, as shown in the following code:

```
VECTOR InterpolatePosition(int object,float t)
  {
  return(Vector(
    InterpolateTable(Animate.data,Animate.cols,
      Animate.step,3*object+1,t),
    InterpolateTable(Animate.data,Animate.cols,
      Animate.step,3*object+2,t),
    InterpolateTable(Animate.data,Animate.cols,
      Animate.step,3*object+3,t))
    );
  }
```

Throughout a sequence, each of the moving objects is advanced in the same way, as listed in the code below:

```
void UpdateObjectPositions(float t)
  {
  VECTOR v;
  Container.bot=InterpolatePosition(cage_bottom,t);
  Container.can=InterpolatePosition(canister   ,t);
  Container.cas=InterpolatePosition(casing     ,t);
  Container.hat=InterpolatePosition(cell_hatch ,t);
  Container.lid=InterpolatePosition(casing_lid ,t);
  Container.plg=InterpolatePosition(casing_plug,t);
  Container.top=InterpolatePosition(cage_top   ,t);
  Container.trk=InterpolatePosition(truck      ,t);
  Crane6       =InterpolatePosition(crane_6ton ,t);
  Crane30      =InterpolatePosition(crane_30ton,t);
  GloveBox     =InterpolatePosition(glove_box  ,t);
  Cask.position=InterpolatePosition(probe_cask ,t);
  Shield[0]    =InterpolatePosition(shield1    ,t);
  Shield[1]    =InterpolatePosition(shield2    ,t);
  Shield[2]    =InterpolatePosition(shield3    ,t);
  v=InterpolatePosition(crane_6ext ,t);crane6_ext =v.x;
```

```
v=InterpolatePosition(crane_6rig ,t);
crane6_rig =v.x>0.5;
v=InterpolatePosition(crane_30rig,t);
crane30_rig=v.x>0.5;
v=InterpolatePosition(probe_sling,t);
Cask.sling =v.x>0.5;
v=InterpolatePosition(probe_angle,t);
Cask.angle =v.z;
}
```

The initial positions of the objects are set in the following code:

```
void InitializeObjects()
  {
  Animate.step=0;
  memset(Animate.data,0,Animate.cols*Animate.rows
    *sizeof(float));
  PosiObject(cage_bottom,Vector( 12.0F,  0.0F,
    18.0F),FALSE);
  PosiObject(canister   ,Vector( 31.8F,-18.6F,
    30.1F),FALSE);
  PosiObject(casing     ,Vector(  6.0F,  0.0F,
    18.0F),FALSE);
  PosiObject(casing_lid ,Vector(  6.0F,  7.8F,
    18.0F),FALSE);
  PosiObject(casing_plug,Vector(  6.0F,  0.0F,
    18.0F),FALSE);
  PosiObject(cage_top   ,Vector(  6.0F,  0.0F,
    38.0F),FALSE);
  PosiObject(cell_hatch ,Vector( 31.8F, -0.4F,
    30.1F),FALSE);
  PosiObject(crane_6ton ,Vector(125.0F, 32.0F,
     2.0F),FALSE);
  PosiObject(crane_30ton,Vector(  3.0F, 29.0F,
     9.0F),FALSE);
  PosiObject(probe_angle,Vector(  0.0F,  0.0F,
    90.0F),FALSE);
  PosiObject(probe_cask ,Vector( 29.1F,  1.0F,
    13.5F),FALSE);
  PosiObject(truck      ,Vector(-20.0F,  0.0F,
    28.0F),FALSE);
  PosiObject(glove_box  ,Vector(GloveBoxPositions[
    active_tank],-12.0F,31.5F),FALSE);
  PosiObject(shield1    ,Vector(GloveBoxPositions[
    shield_position[
    active_tank][0]],-14.0F,31.5F),FALSE);
  PosiObject(shield2    ,Vector(GloveBoxPositions[
    shield_position[active_tank][1]],
    -14.0F,31.5F),FALSE);
  PosiObject(shield3    ,Vector(GloveBoxPositions[
    shield_position[active_tank][2]],-14.0F,
```

```
      31.5F),FALSE);
   NextStep();
   }
```

The animations are also initialized in an allocated list, as shown below:

```
void InitializeAnimation()
   {
   Animate.cols=1+3*things;
   Animate.rows=100;
   Animate.data=allocate(__LINE__,Animate.rows
      *Animate.cols,sizeof(float));
   Animate.high=allocate(__LINE__,Animate.cols,
      sizeof(float));
   Animate.lift=allocate(__LINE__,Animate.cols,
      sizeof(float));
   Animate.high[cage_bottom]= 5.3F;
   Animate.high[canister    ]= 8.5F;
   Animate.high[casing       ]= 9.2F;
   Animate.high[casing_lid  ]= 1.1F;
   Animate.high[casing_plug]= 0.4F;
   Animate.high[cage_top    ]= 4.8F;
   Animate.high[cell_hatch  ]= 0.4F;
   Animate.high[crane_6ton  ]= 2.0F;
   Animate.high[crane_30ton]= 4.5F;
   Animate.high[glove_box   ]= 6.0F;
   Animate.high[shield1      ]= 2.0F;
   Animate.high[shield2      ]= 2.0F;
   Animate.high[shield3      ]= 2.0F;
   Animate.high[truck        ]=11.4F;
   Animate.lift[cage_bottom]= 0.0F;
   Animate.lift[canister    ]= 0.0F;
   Animate.lift[casing       ]=-0.8F;
   Animate.lift[casing_lid  ]= 0.0F;
   Animate.lift[casing_plug]= 0.0F;
   Animate.lift[cage_top    ]=-5.5F;
   Animate.lift[cell_hatch  ]= 0.0F;
   Animate.lift[crane_6ton  ]= 0.7F;
   Animate.lift[crane_30ton]= 2.5F;
   Animate.lift[glove_box   ]= 0.0F;
   Animate.lift[shield1      ]= 1.0F;
   Animate.lift[shield2      ]= 1.0F;
   Animate.lift[shield3      ]= 1.0F;
   Animate.lift[truck        ]= 0.0F;
   InitializeObjects();
   UpdateObjectPositions(0);
   }
```

The two cranes slide along the tracks in both X and Z while transporting, lifting, and lowering, the cask.

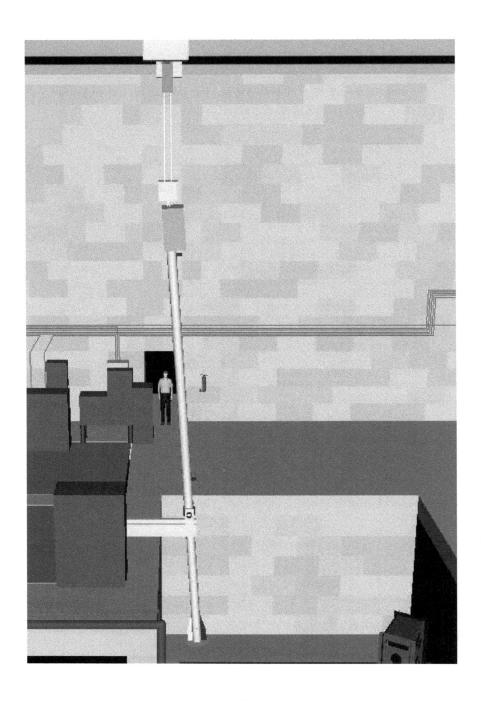

Chapter 10. Track Motion

The clearest and most concise example of track motion is the rollercoaster example that comes with the OpenGL SDK. You can also find it in the online archive accompanying *3D Rendering in Windows* in folder examples\coaster. One position is shown below:

This is a wonderfully complex, yet straightforward implementation of an articulating wheeled carriage on an elaborate track reminiscent of many amusement park attractions. The wheels even rotate to add further realism. The camera follows the carriage along the track and the sky moves with the camera to give a perception of distance.

There are three code modules (coaster.c, defrc.c, and matrix.c) that make up this model. The first is the main program and the last facilitates the needed vector calculations. The second code (defrc.c) defines the track using a unique script, which is so very remarkable and creative[1]—a real treat compared to some

---

[1] If you ever find out who wrote this, please send me an Email so that I can properly credit the creative genius!

lengthy numeric data statements, such as this author has employed in so many models. The track description is so delightful that we will begin there. Definition takes the form of sequential text statements. Those beginning with an asterisk are comments. Below is an excerpt:

```c
char*coaster[]={
   "*first (all gentle) slope",
   "pitch 16 10",
   "wait 10",
   "*weather rectify",
   "pitch 0 10",
   "wait 100",
   "pitch -16 10",
   "wait 10",
   "pitch 0 10",
   "wait 10",
   "*",
   "*first bend (right)",
   "*begin turning",
   "alignment 40 30",
   "wait 20",
   "*initial curve",
   "heading -45 10",
   "wait 10",
   "*end screw",
   "alignment 0 30",
   "wait 79",
   "*turn out early",
   "alignment -10 30",
   "wait 10",
   "*end bend",
   "heading 0 10",
   "wait 20",
   "*end printouts",
   "alignment 0 10",
   "wait 160",
   "*",
   "*second turn (right)",
   "*start turning",
   "alignment 10 10",
   "wait 20",
   "*initial curve",
   "heading -45 10",
   "wait 10",
   "*end screw",
   "alignment 0 30",
   "wait 79",
   "*turn out early",
   "alignment -40 30",
and so forth...,NULL};
```

Let us next examine the very compact code that interprets these statements. It is surrounded by a for() statement that advances through the list until reaching a NULL text pointer. The keywords (pitch, alignment, heading, roll, and wait) are contained in the scanf() statement, which illustrates the most excellent compactness of the C programming language compared to all others.

```
for(in=0;coaster[in];in++)
  {
  if(coaster[in][0]=='*')
    continue;
  else if(sscanf(coaster[in],"pitch %lf %d",&a,&i))
    {
    pitch.speed=(a-pitch.value)/i;
    pitch.steps=i;
    }
  else if(sscanf(coaster[in],"alignment %lf %d",
    &a,&i))
    {
    alignment.speed=(a-alignment.value)/i;
    alignment.steps=i;
    }
  else if(sscanf(coaster[in],"heading %lf %d",&a,&i))
    {
    heading.speed=(a-heading.value)/i;
    heading.steps=i;
    }
  else if(sscanf(coaster[in],"roll %lf %d",&a,&i))
    {
    roll.speed=(a-roll.value)/i;
    roll.steps=i;
    }
  else if(sscanf(coaster[in],"wait %d",&i))
    etc...
  }
```

Lists are used in the same pattern of function calls to render each wheel.

```
void display_wheel(float w)
  {
  int ww=w;
  glPopMatrix();
  glPushMatrix();
  glTranslatef(x[ww],y[ww],z[ww]);
  glRotatef(r3[ww]*180/M_PI,0.0,0.0,1.0);
  glRotatef(-r2[ww]*180/M_PI,0.0,1.0,0.0);
  glRotatef(r1[ww]*180/M_PI,1.0,0.0,0.0);
  glTranslatef(-0.15*(w-ww),0.8,0.0);
  glRotatef(-w,0.0,0.0,1.0);
  glCallList(2);
  glEnd();
  }
```

Here is a different view of the elaborate track:

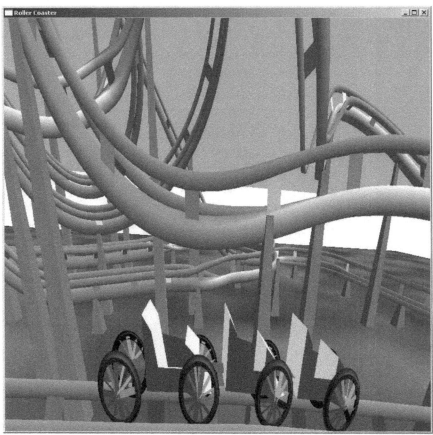

Track motion is also used in the MSRE example with the two cranes and also the truck that removes the contaminated waste in it's special container. The two cranes travel along two different XZ tracks, which must avoid each other plus only one can be used at a time.

```
VECTOR Crane6;
float crane6_ext;
int crane6_rig;
void ParkCrane6()
  {
  Crane6.x=125.F;
  Crane6.y= 32.F;
  Crane6.z=  2.F;
  }
```

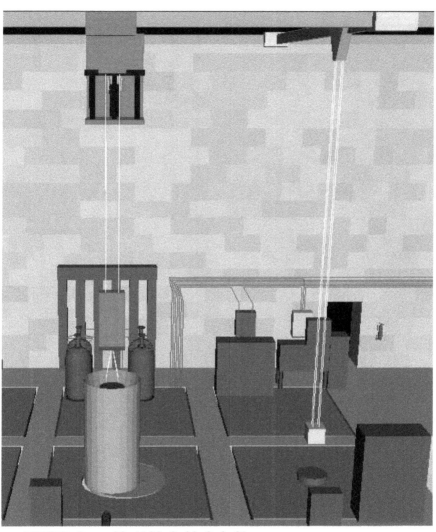

```
VECTOR Crane30={120.0,29.0,3.0};
int crane30_rig;
void ParkCrane30()
  {
  Crane30.x=120.0;
  Crane30.y= 29.0;
  Crane30.z=  3.0;
  }
```

Chapter 11. Reflecting Motion

For reflecting motion we consider Brian Paul's bounce demo, which is included with the Mesa SDK (and can also be found in the online archive). The scene contains a ball, a floor, and a wall—simple enough objects (sphere and two flat planes). The basic scene is shown below:

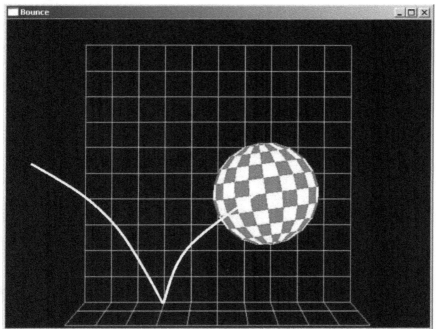

The checkerboard pattern adds some complexity but the wall and ball are easily drawn without resorting to lists. Only the position and orientation as a function of time are needed. While it is straightforward enough to describe simple harmonic motion with a few trig functions, this implementation is even less complicated. Brian Paul's bounce demo uses an initial velocity vector followed by simple reflection. When the ball reaches a boundary of the invisible box (Xmin,Ymin) to (Xmax,Ymax), the velocity components are reversed, sending it back in the other direction. The code is quite simple:

```
void idle(void)
  {
  static float vel0=-100.0;
  Zrot+=Zstep;
  Xpos+=Xvel;
  if(Xpos>=Xmax)
    {
    Xpos=Xmax;
    Xvel=-Xvel;
```

47

```
      Zstep=-Zstep;
      }
  if(Xpos<=Xmin)
      {
      Xpos=Xmin;
      Xvel=-Xvel;
      Zstep=-Zstep;
      }
  Ypos+=Yvel;
  Yvel+=G;
  if(Ypos<Ymin)
      {
      Ypos=Ymin;
      if(vel0==-100.0)
         vel0=fabs(Yvel);
      Yvel=vel0;
      }
  glutPostRedisplay();
  }
```

A similar reflection calculation is used in molecular modeling, as illustrated below:

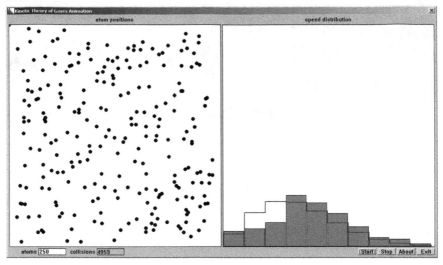

Chapter 12. Bouncing Motion

For bouncing motion we consider Mark Kilgard's reflect example included in the OpenGL SDK (and can also be found in the online archive). While the primary purpose of this example is to demonstrate how to generate a reflected image, the dinosaur also bounces and so we examine it here rather than reinventing the wheel and proliferating unnecessary examples. The typical scene is depicted below:

The vertical position (i.e., bounce) is a simple sine wave:

```
void idle(void)
  {
  static float time;
  time=glutGet(GLUT_ELAPSED_TIME)/500.;
  jump=3.*fabs(sin(time));
  glutPostRedisplay();
  }
```

Constructing the dinosaur by extruding polygons (i.e., making a third dimension from a two-dimensional form). The extrusion setup is straightforward:

```
void makeDinosaur(void)
  {
  extrudeSolidFromPolygon(body, sizeof(body),
    bodyWidth, BODY_SIDE, BODY_EDGE, BODY_WHOLE);
  extrudeSolidFromPolygon(arm, sizeof(arm),
    bodyWidth/4, ARM_SIDE, ARM_EDGE, ARM_WHOLE);
  extrudeSolidFromPolygon(leg, sizeof(leg),
    bodyWidth/2, LEG_SIDE, LEG_EDGE, LEG_WHOLE);
  extrudeSolidFromPolygon(eye, sizeof(eye),
    bodyWidth+0.2, EYE_SIDE, EYE_EDGE, EYE_WHOLE);
  }
```

The function extrudeSolidFromPolygon() function can be used in other models. It transforms each part into a list glNewList(), fills it with calls to glBegin(GL_QUAD_STRIP) and glVertex3f(), and then closes it off with a call to glEnd() and glEndList(). The first glEnd() closes off the glBegin(GL_QUAD_STRIP) and the second closes off the list. The dinosaur is drawn by rendering the lists sequentially:

```
void drawDinosaur(void)
  {
  glPushMatrix();
  glTranslatef(0., jump, 0.);
  glMaterialfv(GL_FRONT, GL_DIFFUSE, skinColor);
  glCallList(BODY_WHOLE);
  glPushMatrix();
  glTranslatef(0., 0., bodyWidth);
  glCallList(ARM_WHOLE);
  glCallList(LEG_WHOLE);
  glTranslatef(0., 0., -bodyWidth-bodyWidth/4);
  glCallList(ARM_WHOLE);
  glTranslatef(0., 0., -bodyWidth/4);
  glCallList(LEG_WHOLE);
  glTranslatef(0., 0., bodyWidth/2-0.1);
  glMaterialfv(GL_FRONT, GL_DIFFUSE, eyeColor);
  glCallList(EYE_WHOLE);
  glPopMatrix();
  glPopMatrix();
  }
```

While reflections are not the main focus of this text, it is worth noting here with this example that the reflection is actually a second dinosaur, drawn upside down and backwards with altered lighting. There are many helpful comments in the source code (reflect.c), describing the details required, including back face culling and how the orientation flips and must be reversed.

Chapter 13. Sliding Motion

The first example of sliding motion we will consider is the chess demo written by Henk Kok that comes with the GLUT distribution package. The files can also be found in the online archive in the folder examples\OpenGL\chess. Not only do the pieces slide around, when one is captured, it sinks into the board. There are seven files that accomplish the task of rendering this model.

- main.c sets up the application and launches the GLUT context
- animate.c moves the pieces
- chess.c defines the board and pieces
- chess.h declares the functions and variables
- pathplan.c defines the available path for a piece
- texture.c defines textures (e.g., marble)
- chess.inp contains the moves in succinct notation

The notation in chess.inp is interesting. This is an excerpt: d2d4, g8f6, c2c4, g7g6, b1c3, f8g7, e2e4, d7d6, ... The texture is not visible in the following snapshot:

As we have seen before, lists are used to facilitate the process. The following is an example of building a list for the king (konig) and queen (dame):

```
glNewList(KONING+8*i,GL_COMPILE);
do_koning();
```

```
width[KONING+8*i]=bwidth;
height[KONING+8*i]=bheight;
glEndList();
glNewList(DAME+8*i,GL_COMPILE);
do_dame();
width[DAME+8*i]=bwidth;
height[DAME+8*i]=bheight;
glEndList();
```

The pieces are drawn at the proper location by first translating, then rotating. The position and view are preserved by pushing and then popping the transformation matrix.

```
glPushMatrix();
glTranslatef(x-1.,((x==CX2&&y==CY2)?CZ2:0.),8.-y);
glScalef(1.2,1.2,1.2);
glCallList(pc+list[0]);
glPopMatrix();
```

The following section of code is illustrative:

```
#define MOVE_FRAC 8
switch(path[X][Y])
  {
  case NORTH:     NY--;break;
  case SOUTH:     NY++;break;
  case WEST:      NX--;break;
  case EAST:      NX++;break;
  case NORTHWEST:NX--;NY--;break;
  case NORTHEAST:NX++;NY--;break;
  case SOUTHWEST:NX--;NY++;break;
  case SOUTHEAST:NX+-;NY++;break;
  }
CX1=(X*(MOVE_FRAC-frac)+NX*frac)/MOVE_FRAC;
CY1=(Y*(MOVE_FRAC-frac)+NY*frac)/MOVE_FRAC;
```

Here we see the eight possible directions (four sides plus four corners) a piece can move linked to the change in XY position. Movement is broken up into eight steps (see MOVE_FRAC definition above). These are performed sequentially. The end result appears to be a smooth sliding motion. The rate arises from a combination of the default idle timer and the processing duration. There is also a wait or skip variable (extern int speed) that can be adjusted with the UP and DOWN keys. Even this simplistic process produces a satisfactory result, indicating that complicated stepping schemes may not always be necessary when constructing such models.

The next sliding motion we will consider is that present in Kevin Smith's glpuzzle demp, which is included in the OpenGL SDK (may also be found in the online archive). This application slides pieces in response to mouse movement using the trackball utility files (trackball.c and trackball.h). The scene is quite simple to encode and render:

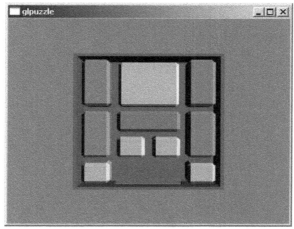

Perhaps the most complex part of this code is keeping track of where the pieces are and what moves are legitimate. This is done in the main source code. Not surprisingly, this is handled in function canmove() with assistance from canmove0(). There is also a function to determine which piece has been selected: selectpiece() as well as one to remove a piece: nukepiece(). Piece repositioning begins with function: grabpiece(). You will find this code quite readable and easy to follow with the functions named so naturally. The shapes and lighting are uncomplicated, which keeps focus on the selection and movement.

Knight's Tour

The knight's tour demo also slides the pieces across the board. The *tour* describes 64 sequential moves, landing on each square only once. The algorithm is quite simple and surprisingly effective. It uses a stack to keep previous partially successful sequences. When a path ends in failure, the stack is popped and the last partially successful one is continued. At each juncture, the move having the largest number of potential next moves beyond that space is selected. The following section of code implements this logic:

```
int MoveOK(int x,int y)
  {
  if(x<0)
    return(0);
  if(x>7)
    return(0);
  if(y<0)
    return(0);
  if(y>7)
    return(0);
  if(board[y][x])
    return(0);
```

53

```
      return(1);
      }
int Moves(int x,int y)
    {
    int i,n;
    for(n=i=0;i<8;i++)
      n+=MoveOK(x+move[i].x,y+move[i].y);
    return(n);
    }
int EndTour(int x1,int y1)
    {
    int i,m=0,n1,n2,x2,x3,y2,y3;
    memset(board,0,sizeof(board));
    board[y1][x1]=1;
    Tour[0].x=x1;
    Tour[0].y=y1;
    while(1)
      {
      n1=9;
      for(i=0;i<8;i++)
        {
        x2=x1+move[i].x;
        y2=y1+move[i].y;
        if(!MoveOK(x2,y2))
          continue;
        if(m==62)
          {
          x3=x2;
          y3=y2;
          break;
          }
        n2=Moves(x2,y2);
        board[y2][x2]=0;
        if(n2<1||n2>=n1)
          continue;
        x3=x2;
        y3=y2;
        n1=n2;
        }
      if(n1==9&&m!=62)
        return(0);
      m++;
      x1=x3;
      y1=y3;
      board[y3][x3]=m+1;
      Tour[m].x=x3;
      Tour[m].y=y3;
      if(m==63)
        break;
```

```
      }
   return(m);
   }
void BeginTour(int s)
   {
   int x1,y1;
   x1=(int)(Object[s][0]-'A');
   y1=(int)(Object[s][1]-'1');
   if(EndTour(x1,y1))
      {
      for(pending_tour=1;pending_tour<=64;pending_tour++)
         {
         Piece[1].col=Tour[pending_tour-1].x;
         Piece[1].row=Tour[pending_tour-1].y;
         RePaint();
         }
      }
   else
      MessageBox(hMain,"knight's tour was not
      successful","algorithm failure",MB_APPLMODAL|MB_OK);
   }
```

Function MoveOK() returns 0 or 1 (yes or no). Function Moves() counts the number of potential next moves. BeginTour() initiates the process. EndTour() finds the path. Function RePaint() moves the knight after the path has been loaded into an array. The tour is rendered by the following instructions:

```
void RenderTour()
   {
   int i,n;
   float a,r=0.0125,x1,x2,x3,x4,x5,x6,y=0.0125,
      z1,z2,z3,z4,z5,z6;
   glDisable(GL_TEXTURE_2D);
   glColor(0xFF0000);
   glBegin(GL_QUADS);
   glNormal3f(0.,1.,0.);
   x2=Brd[Tour[0].y];
   z2=Brd[Tour[0].x];
   n=min(64,pending_tour);
   for(i=1;i<n;i++)
      {
      x1=x2;
      z1=z2;
      x2=Brd[Tour[i].y];
      z2=Brd[Tour[i].x];
      a=atan2(z2-z1,x2-x1);
      x3=x1-r*sin(a);
      x4=x2-r*sin(a);
      x5=x1+r*sin(a);
      x6=x2+r*sin(a);
```

```
      z3=z1+r*cos(a);
      z4=z2+r*cos(a);
      z5=z1-r*cos(a);
      z6=z2-r*cos(a);
      glVertex3f(x3,y,z3);
      glVertex3f(x4,y,z4);
      glVertex3f(x6,y,z6);
      glVertex3f(x5,y,z5);
      }
   glEnd();
   }
```

Different paths result depending on the initial square. The end result is shown below:

Chapter 14. Combining Simple Motions

The Olympic ring demo included in the OpenGL SDK is simple and easy to follow. The rings are a torus and are rendered each in turn with quadrangles by the following function:

```
void FillTorus(float rc,int numc,float rt,int numt)
  {
  int i,j,k;
  double s,t,x,y,z;
  for(i=0;i<numc;i++)
    {
    glBegin(GL_QUAD_STRIP);
    for(j=0;j<=numt;j++)
      {
      for(k=1;k>=0;k--)
        {
        s=(i+k)%numc+0.5;
        t=j%numt;
        x=cos(t*2*M_PI/numt)*cos(s*2*M_PI/numc);
        y=sin(t*2*M_PI/numt)*cos(s*2*M_PI/numc);
        z=sin(s*2*M_PI/numc);
        glNormal3f(x,y,z);
        x=(rt+rc*cos(s*2*M_PI/numc))*cos(t*2*M_PI/numt);
        y=(rt+rc*cos(s*2*M_PI/numc))*sin(t*2*M_PI/numt);
        z=rc*sin(s*2*M_PI/numc);
        glVertex3f(x,y,z);
        }
      }
    glEnd();
    }
  }
```

The initial ring positions and rotations are defined during setup within function InitializeRings().

```
for(i=0;i<RINGS;i++)
  {
  offsets[i][0]=Rand();
  offsets[i][1]=Rand();
  offsets[i][2]=Rand();
  angs[i]=260.*Rand();
  rotAxis[i][0]=Rand();
  rotAxis[i][1]=Rand();
  rotAxis[i][2]=Rand();
  iters[i]=(deviation*Rand()+60.);
  }
```

That these are random isn't material, only that they are removed from their final positions, which are also defined in this same function:

```
dests[BLUERING][0]=-spacing;
dests[BLUERING][1]=top_y;
```

```
dests[BLUERING][2]=top_z;
dests[BLACKRING][0]=0.;
dests[BLACKRING][1]=top_y;
dests[BLACKRING][2]=top_z;
dests[REDRING][0]=spacing;
dests[REDRING][1]=top_y;
dests[REDRING][2]=top_z;
dests[YELLOWRING][0]=-spacing/2.;
dests[YELLOWRING][1]=bottom_y;
dests[YELLOWRING][2]=bottom_z;
dests[GREENRING][0]=spacing/2.;
dests[GREENRING][1]=bottom_y;
dests[GREENRING][2]=bottom_z;
```

The initial position of the rings is shown in this first figure:

The transition is then from the initial to the final destinations in steps. The number of steps for each transition is nominally random and stored in array iters[]. This randomness is also immaterial to the end result, although it does provide some variety. As the random numbers are not seeded, these will always be the same. The iterative transition is performed in such a way as to appear rapid at first, slowing as each ring's destination is approached. The following code accomplishes this effect:

```
float Clamp(int iters_left,float t)
  {
  if(iters_left<3)
    return(0.);
  return(iters_left-2)*t/iters_left;
  }
```

58

```
for(i=0;i<RINGS;i++)
  {
  if(iters[i])
    {
    for(j=0;j<3;j++)
      offsets[i][j]=Clamp(iters[i],offsets[i][j]);
    angs[i]=Clamp(iters[i],angs[i]);
    iters[i]--;
    }
  }
```

The final result is shown in this second figure:

Lorenz Attractor

The next combined simple motion we will consider is that of the Lorenz attractor demo written by Aaron Ferrucci and included in the OpenGL SDK (may also be found in the online archive). The following description accompanies this demo:

> This program shows some particles stuck in a Lorenz attractor (the parameters used are r=28,b=8/3,sigma=10). The eye is attracted to the red particle, with a force directly proportionate to distance. A command line puts the whole mess inside a box made of hexagons. I think this helps to maintain the illusion of 3 dimensions, but it can slow things down. Other options allow you to play with the redraw rate and the number of new lines per redraw. So you can customize it to the speed of your machine.

The biggest difference between this example and the previous ones is that the motion follows a specific pattern described by the physics controlling the motion of the particles. The position of the particles is calculated at each time step in the following function:

```
void move_eye(void)
  {
  /* first move the eye */
  eyev[0]+=gravity*(rv[rp][0]-eyex[0]);
  eyev[1]+=gravity*(rv[rp][1]-eyex[1]);
```

```
eyev[2]+=gravity*(rv[rp][2]-eyex[2]);
/* adjust position using new velocity */
eyex[0]+=eyev[0]*dt;
eyex[1]+=eyev[1]*dt;
eyex[2]+=eyev[2]*dt;
/* move the lookat point */
/* it catches up to the red point if it's moving
  slowly enough */
eyel[0]+=LG*(rv[rp][0]-eyel[0]);
eyel[1]+=LG*(rv[rp][1]-eyel[1]);
eyel[2]+=LG*(rv[rp][2]-eyel[2]);
/* change view */
gluLookAt(eyex[0],eyex[1],eyex[2],eyel[0],
  eyel[1],eyel[2],0,1,0);
}
```

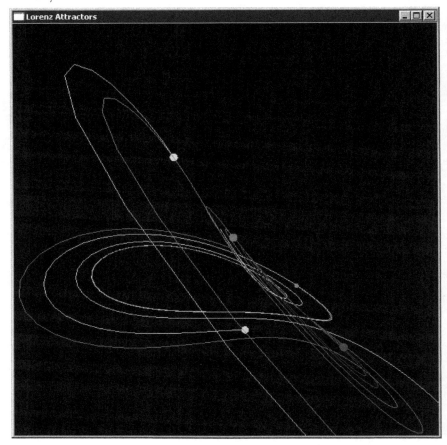

The GLUT function call gluLookAt() facilitates the necessary adjustments to give a desirable overall effect of motion and viewpoint. The preceding figure is typical of the resulting animation. Notice that the main rendering function (listed below) draws the particles and also the trails as curves of the same color.

```
void redraw(void)
    {
    glClear(GL_COLOR_BUFFER_BIT|GL_DEPTH_BUFFER_BIT);
    if(hexflag)
      draw_hexcube();
    glColor3f(1.0,0.0,0.0);
    drawLines(rp,rv);
    sphdraw(rv[rp]);
    glColor3f(0.0,0.0,1.0);
    drawLines(bp,bv);
    sphdraw(bv[bp]);
    glColor3f(0.0,1.0,0.0);
    drawLines(gp,gv);
    sphdraw(gv[gp]);
    glColor3f(1.0,0.0,1.0);
    drawLines(yp,yv);
    sphdraw(yv[yp]);
    glColor3f(0.0,1.0,1.0);
    drawLines(mp,mv);
    sphdraw(mv[mp]);
    glutSwapBuffers();
    }
```

The particles are drawn using a list for compactness:

```
void sphdraw(float args[3])
    {
    glPushMatrix();
    glTranslatef(args[0],args[1],args[2]);
    glCallList(asphere);
    glPopMatrix();
    }
```

The view is saved and restored by pushing it onto the stack before rendering and then popping it off before continuing. The track lines are added by this function:

```
void next_line(float v[][3],int *p)
    {
    dx=sigma*(v[*p][1]-v[*p][0])*dt;
    dy=(r*v[*p][0]-v[*p][1]+v[*p][0]*v[*p][2])*dt;
    dz=(v[*p][0]*v[*p][1]+b*v[*p][2])*dt;
    v[(*p+1)&POINTMASK][0]=v[*p][0]+dx;
    v[(*p+1)&POINTMASK][1]=v[*p][1]+dy;
    v[(*p+1)&POINTMASK][2]=v[*p][2]-dz;
    *p=(*p+1)&POINTMASK;
    }
```

The track lines are drawn in four steps by the following function:

```
#define LINE_STEP 4
void drawLines(int index,float array[POINTMASK][3])
  {
  int p;
  int i;
  p=(index+1)&POINTMASK;
  i=LINE_STEP-(p%LINE_STEP);
  if(i==LINE_STEP)
    i=0;
  glBegin(GL_LINE_STRIP);
  /* draw points in order from oldest to newest */
  while(p!=index)
    {
    if(i==0)
      {
      glVertex3fv(array[p]);
      i=LINE_STEP;
      }
    i--;
    p=(p+1)&POINTMASK;
    }
  glVertex3fv(array[index]);
  glEnd();
  }
```

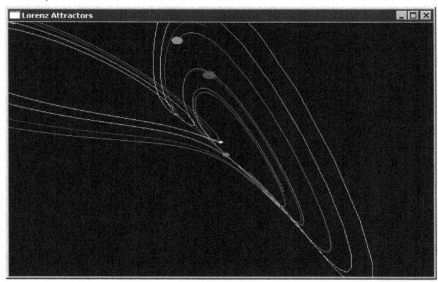

The ETTP demo includes a six-foot man to give scale and proportion:

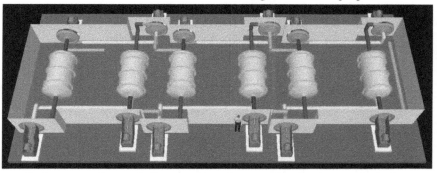

It also uses colors to indicate stages of preparation for decommissioning:

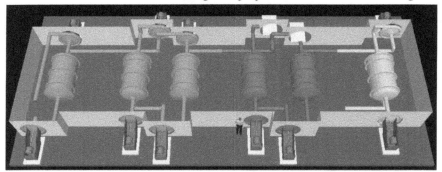

The parts are disassembled in order using a combination of sliding and rotating motions. This animated model was used for training in preparation for disassembly.

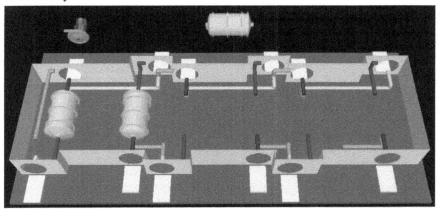

The steps to remove one of the electric motors is shown in the following code segment:

```
int RemoveMotor()
  {
  float s;
  static float motor[]={
     0.04F,  0.04F,
    -0.89F,  0.40F,
    -0.43F,  0.35F,
    -0.28F,  0.40F,
     0.18F,  0.35F,
     0.33F,  0.40F,
     0.80F,  0.35F,
     0.89F, -0.40F,
     0.43F, -0.35F,
     0.28F, -0.40F,
    -0.18F, -0.35F,
    -0.33F, -0.40F,
    -0.80F, -0.35F,
     FLT_MAX};
  while(dismantle.motor.i<12)
    {
    if(!(_show[dismantle.motor.i]&_motor))
      {
      dismantle.motor.i++;
      continue;
      }
    if(dismantle.motor.j>=dismantle.motor.n)
      {
      dismantle.motor.j=0;
      dismantle.motor.k++;
      if(dismantle.motor.k==1)
        {
        _move[dismantle.motor.i]|=_motor|_mount
          |_shaft|_compr;
        memset(&_Move,0,sizeof(_Move));
        dismantle.motor.dz=(float)(fabs(motor[
          2*(dismantle.motor.i+1)+1])-0.6);
        dismantle.motor.n=(int)max(1,
          fabs(dismantle.motor.dz)/0.05)+1;
        s=max(motor[0],motor[1])/2;
        dismantle.motor.dz/=dismantle.motor.n*s;
        }
      else if(dismantle.motor.k==2)
        {
        dismantle.motor.dx=-sneg((float)(1.2+motor[
        2*(dismantle.motor.i+1)]),dismantle.motor.i<6);
        dismantle.motor.n=(int)max(1,
          fabs(dismantle.motor.dx)/0.05)+1;
```

```
            s=max(motor[0],motor[1])/2;
            dismantle.motor.dx/=dismantle.motor.n*s;
            }
        else
            {
            _move[dismantle.motor.i]^=_motor|_mount|
              _shaft|_compr;
            _show[dismantle.motor.i]|=_motor|_mount|
              _shaft|_compr;
            _show[dismantle.motor.i]^=_motor|_mount|
              _shaft|_compr;
            dismantle.motor.i++;
            dismantle.motor.j=0;
            dismantle.motor.k=0;
            dismantle.motor.n=0;
            continue;
            }
        }
    if(dismantle.motor.k==1)
      _Move.z+=dismantle.motor.dz;
    else if(dismantle.motor.k==2)
      _Move.x+=dismantle.motor.dx;
    SetWindowText(hStat,"REMOVING MOTORS AND
    COMPRESSORS");
    RePaint();
    dismantle.motor.j++;
    return(0);
    }
  return(1);
  }
```

The procedure to remove one of the pipes is much simpler:

```
int RemovePipe()
  {
  while(dismantle.pipe.i<24)
    {
    if(dismantle.pipe.i<12)
      {
      if(!(_show[dismantle.pipe.i]&_pipe1))
        {
        dismantle.pipe.i++;
        continue;
        }
      }
    else
      {
      if(!(_show[dismantle.pipe.i-12]&_pipe2))
        {
        dismantle.pipe.i++;
        continue;
```

```
        }
      }
    if(dismantle.pipe.i<12)
      _show[dismantle.pipe.i]^=_pipe1;
    else
      _show[dismantle.pipe.i-12]^=_pipe2;
    SetWindowText(hStat,"REMOVING PIPES");
    RePaint();
    dismantle.pipe.i++;
    return(0);
    }
  return(1);
  }
```

Each of these utilizes a stepping motion along a predetermined path from the current position to the final one, which is out of view. The camera position and point of view of the observer can be changed during this process in order to give any number of perspectives on the same motion. This was particularly helpful during the dismantling. The program originally kept an inventory of components and the state of each, including the name of the user, the computer used, and the time of any changes. All of the changes could be reversed or advanced in order to produce a view representing the state of the entire system at any time during the decommissioning process.

Chapter 15. Swimming Motion

Our example of swimming motion is Mark Kilgard's Atlantis demo, which comes with the GLUT distribution package. The code is conveniently broken down into sections:

- atlantis.c: the main program
- dolphin.c: defines the dolphin object
- shark.c: defines the shark object
- whale.c: defines the whale object
- swim.c: defines the swimming motions

The swim code module also includes a function SharkMiss() that avoids collisions and also provides the appearance of fleeing the denizens. As is the case with all of Kilgard's codes, Atlantis is clearly written with meaningful function and variable names like fish->attack and SHARKSPEED. There are even two object names (momwhale and babywhale) of type fishrec.The angles are named psi and theta. The position calculations are also easily identified:

```
x=fish->xt-fish->x;
y=fish->yt-fish->y;
z=fish->zt-fish->z;
```

The final result is quite satisfactory:

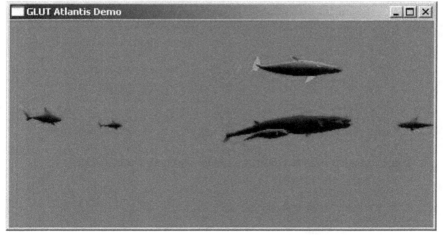

The smaller dolphins even flap faster than the larger whales, adding to the realism. Another detail adding to the realism is articulation and segmentation, controlled by the natural variables:

```
fish->vtail+=(fish->dtheta-fish->vtail)/10;
if(fish->vtail>0.5)
   fish->vtail=0.5;
else if(fish->vtail<-0.5)
```

```
fish->vtail=-0.5;
segup=thrash*fish->vtail;
```

Here we see a closer view of mama and baby whale. Notice the articulating segments indicated by the red lines.

All of the fish move about the center in a circular motion, much like the Moon orbiting the Earth. They move at different speeds and also articulate (see variables involving "thrash"). The whale orientation and position is updated by the following code:

```
void WhalePilot(fishRec*fish)
  {
  fish->phi=-20.;
  fish->theta=0.;
  fish->psi-=0.5;
  fish->x+=WHALESPEED*fish->v*
    cos(fish->psi/RAD)*cos(fish->theta/RAD);
  fish->y+=WHALESPEED*fish->v*
    sin(fish->psi/RAD)*cos(fish->theta/RAD);
  fish->z+=WHALESPEED*fish->v*sin(fish->theta/RAD);
  }
```

Some variation is added though a random number comparison:

```
if(rand()%100>98)
  sign=1-sign;
fish->psi+=sign;
if(fish->psi>180.)
  fish->psi-=360.;
if(fish->psi<-180.)
  fish->psi+=360.;
```

The other fish lurch forward (i.e., "spurt") when too close to a shark:

```
if(fish->attack)
  {
  if(fish->v<1.1)
```

68

```
      fish->spurt=1;
   if(fish->spurt)
      fish->v+=0.2;
   if(fish->v>5.)
      fish->spurt=0;
   if((fish->v>1.)&&(!fish->spurt))
      fish->v-=0.2;
   }
```

There is even a large-scale variation to assure escape from a shark encounter:

```
void SharkMiss(int i)
   {
   int j;
   float avoid,thetal;
   float X,Y,Z,R;
   for(j=0; j<NUM_SHARKS; j++)
      {
      if(j!=i)
         {
         X=sharks[j].x-sharks[i].x;
         Y=sharks[j].y-sharks[i].y;
         Z=sharks[j].z-sharks[i].z;
         R=sqrt(X*X+Y*Y+Z*Z);
         avoid=1.;
         thetal=sharks[i].theta;
         if(R<SHARKSIZE)
            {
            if(Z>0.)
               sharks[i].theta-=avoid;
            else
               sharks[i].theta+=avoid;
            }
         sharks[i].dtheta+=(sharks[i].theta-thetal);
         }
      }
   }
```

Not only are Kilgard's programs well written and efficient, they clear, rather than obfuscated, as seems so often to be the case with much sample code. The function driving the animation, indicated by a call to the GLUT utility function glutIdleFunc(Animate), couldn't be any more concise:

```
void Animate(void)
   {
   int i;
   static now,then=-1;
   if(then==-1)
      then=GetTickCount();
   else
```

```
  {
  now=GetTickCount();
  if(now<=then)
    return;
  then=now;
  }
for(i=0;i<NUM_SHARKS;i++)
  {
  SharkPilot(&sharks[i]);
  SharkMiss(i);
  }
WhalePilot(&dolph);
dolph.phi++;
glutPostRedisplay();
WhalePilot(&momWhale);
momWhale.phi++;
WhalePilot(&babyWhale);
babyWhale.phi++;
  }
```

Chapter 16. Stretching Motion

Our example of stretching motion, morph3d.c, was developed by Brian Paul and Marcelo Vianna and comes with the Mesa SDK (also included in the online archive accompanying *3D Rendering in Windows*). This demo consists of five geometric shapes (tetrahedron, cube (hexahedron), octahedron, dodecahedron, and icosahedron), which are drawn on top of each other. The conglomerate swirls about on the screen inside a box so that it is sometimes closer and sometimes farther from the observer.

The shapes are also distorted as time progresses. The distortions are cyclical, so that the appearance is stretched and squished over and over again. As one of the five shapes is stretched and the others squished, that one becomes dominant, appearing to engulf the others. Gross movement is simple and has been covered in previous chapters. The surfaces (polygons) are simply colored, making the primary focus of this demo the cyclical distortions.

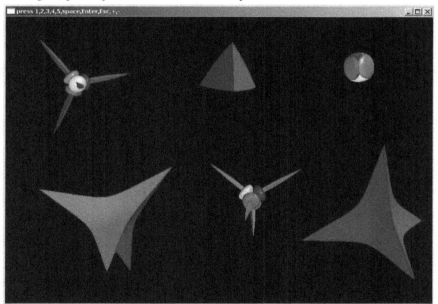

All of the polyhedral objects are drawn one face at a time, rotating and translating the polygons as needed to obtain the desired undistorted shape. The tetrahedron is the simplest, so it will be listed here. The others are similar with more calls.

```
void draw_cube(void)
   {
   GLuint list;
   list=glGenLists(1);
   glNewList(list,GL_COMPILE);
```

```
      SQUARE(2,seno,edgedivisions,0.5);
      glEndList();
      glMaterialfv(GL_FRONT_AND_BACK,GL_DIFFUSE,
        MaterialColor[0]);
      glCallList(list);
      glRotatef(cubeangle,1,0,0);
      glMaterialfv(GL_FRONT_AND_BACK,GL_DIFFUSE,
        MaterialColor[1]);
      glCallList(list);
      glRotatef(cubeangle,1,0,0);
      glMaterialfv(GL_FRONT_AND_BACK,GL_DIFFUSE,
        MaterialColor[2]);
      glCallList(list);
      glRotatef(cubeangle,1,0,0);
      glMaterialfv(GL_FRONT_AND_BACK,GL_DIFFUSE,
        MaterialColor[3]);
      glCallList(list);
      glRotatef(cubeangle,0,1,0);
      glMaterialfv(GL_FRONT_AND_BACK,GL_DIFFUSE,
        MaterialColor[4]);
      glCallList(list);
      glRotatef(2*cubeangle,0,1,0);
      glMaterialfv(GL_FRONT_AND_BACK,GL_DIFFUSE,
        MaterialColor[5]);
      glCallList(list);
      glDeleteLists(list,1);
      }
```

Each of the faces is a list glCallList() consisting of a single distorted polygon. The same list is used glGenLists(1) and the colors are changed before each face glMaterialfV() with MaterialColor[face_index]. Each distorted triangle is generated in the following function:

```
void TRIANGLE(GLfloat Edge,GLfloat Amp,
    int Divisions,GLfloat Z)
  {
  GLfloat Xf,Yf,Xa,Yb,Xf2,Yf2;
  GLfloat Factor,Factor1,Factor2;
  GLfloat VertX,VertY,VertZ,NeiAX,NeiAY,NeiAZ,
    NeiBX,NeiBY,NeiBZ;
  GLfloat Ax,Ay,Bx;
  int Ri,Ti;
  GLfloat Vr=(Edge)*SQRT3/3;
  GLfloat AmpVr2=(Amp)/sqr(Vr);
  GLfloat Zf=(Edge)*(Z);
  Ax=(Edge)*(+0.5/(Divisions)),
    Ay=(Edge)*(-SQRT3/(2*Divisions));
  Bx=(Edge)*(-0.5/(Divisions));
  for(Ri=1;Ri<=(Divisions);Ri++)
    {
```

```
glBegin(GL_TRIANGLE_STRIP);
for(Ti=0;Ti<Ri;Ti++)
  {
  Xf=(float)(Ri-Ti)*Ax+(float)Ti*Bx;
  Yf=Vr+(float)(Ri-Ti)*Ay+(float)Ti*Ay;
  Xa=Xf+0.001;
  Yb=Yf+0.001;
  Factor=1-(((Xf2=sqr(Xf))+(Yf2=sqr(Yf)))*AmpVr2);
  Factor1=1-((sqr(Xa)+Yf2)*AmpVr2);
  Factor2=1-((Xf2+sqr(Yb))*AmpVr2);
  VertX=Factor*Xf;
  VertY=Factor*Yf;
  VertZ=Factor*Zf;
  NeiAX=Factor1*Xa-VertX;
  NeiAY=Factor1*Yf-VertY;
  NeiAZ=Factor1*Zf-VertZ;
  NeiBX=Factor2*Xf-VertX;
  NeiBY=Factor2*Yb-VertY;
  NeiBZ=Factor2*Zf-VertZ;
  glNormal3f(VectMul(NeiAX,NeiAY,NeiAZ,
    NeiBX,NeiBY,NeiBZ));
  glVertex3f(VertX,VertY,VertZ);
  Xf=(float)(Ri-Ti-1)*Ax+(float)Ti*Bx;
  Yf=Vr+(float)(Ri-Ti-1)*Ay+(float)Ti*Ay;
  Xa=Xf+0.001;
  Yb=Yf+0.001;
  Factor=1-(((Xf2=sqr(Xf))+(Yf2=sqr(Yf)))*AmpVr2);
  Factor1=1-((sqr(Xa)+Yf2)*AmpVr2);
  Factor2=1-((Xf2+sqr(Yb))*AmpVr2);
  VertX=Factor*Xf;
  VertY=Factor*Yf;
  VertZ=Factor*Zf;
  NeiAX=Factor1*Xa-VertX;
  NeiAY=Factor1*Yf-VertY;
  NeiAZ=Factor1*Zf-VertZ;
  NeiBX=Factor2*Xf-VertX;
  NeiBY=Factor2*Yb-VertY;
  NeiBZ=Factor2*Zf-VertZ;
  glNormal3f(VectMul(NeiAX,NeiAY,NeiAZ,
    NeiBX,NeiBY,NeiBZ));
  glVertex3f(VertX,VertY,VertZ);
}
Xf=(float)Ri*Bx;
Yf=Vr+(float)Ri*Ay;
Xa=Xf+0.001;
Yb=Yf+0.001;
Factor=1-(((Xf2=sqr(Xf))+(Yf2=sqr(Yf)))*AmpVr2);
Factor1=1-((sqr(Xa)+Yf2)*AmpVr2);
Factor2=1-((Xf2+sqr(Yb))*AmpVr2);
```

```
VertX=Factor*Xf;
VertY=Factor*Yf;
VertZ=Factor*Zf;
NeiAX=Factor1*Xa-VertX;
NeiAY=Factor1*Yf-VertY;
NeiAZ=Factor1*Zf-VertZ;
NeiBX=Factor2*Xf-VertX;
NeiBY=Factor2*Yb-VertY;
NeiBZ=Factor2*Zf-VertZ;
glNormal3f(VectMul(NeiAX,NeiAY,NeiAZ,
    NeiBX,NeiBY,NeiBZ));
glVertex3f(VertX,VertY,VertZ);
glEnd();
}
}
```

Notice the user-defined number of increments passed as an integer argument, Divisions, and defined at the top of the code in a data statement. The distortion factors (Factor, Factor1, and Factor2) are related by the Pythagorean Theorem in 3D so as to maintain the proper overall shape. The motion is advanced by incrementing variable "step" by 0.05 in the idle function, listed below.

```
void draw(void)
{
glClear(GL_COLOR_BUFFER_BIT|GL_DEPTH_BUFFER_BIT);
glPushMatrix();
glTranslatef(0.,0.,-10.);
glScalef(Scale*WindH/WindW,Scale,Scale);
glTranslatef(2.5*WindW/WindH*sin(step*1.11),
    2.5*cos(step*1.25*1.11),0);
glRotatef(step*100,1,0,0);
glRotatef(step*95,0,1,0);
glRotatef(step*90,0,0,1);
seno=(sin(step)+1./3.)*(4./5.)*Magnitude;
draw_object();
glPopMatrix();
glFlush();
glutSwapBuffers();
step+=0.05;
}
```

Chapter 17. Exploding Motion

For exploding motion we turn to Mark Kilgard's pointburst demo, which is included in the GLUT distribution package (and also in the online archive). As with all of Kilgard's work, this is concise and well written. The code is readable and easily understood. In this demo droplets come bursting across the horizon and bounce along the surface.

The droplet shape is defined in a data statement like a bitmap character:

```
char*circles[]={
  "....xxxx........",
  "..xxxxxxxx......",
  ".xxxxxxxxxx.....",
  ".xxx....xxx.....",
  "xxx......xxx....",
  "xxx......xxx....",
  "xxx......xxx....",
  "xxx......xxx....",
  ".xxx....xxx.....",
  ".xxxxxxxxxx.....",
  "..xxxxxxxx......",
  "....xxxx........",
  "................",
  "................",
  "................",
  "................",};
```

This could easily be changed to some other simple shape. The same could be defined be much fewer hexadecimal integers, as the character strings are transformed into the latter before use by the following code.

```
for(t=0;t<16;t++)
   {
   for(s=0;s<16;s++)
      {
      if(circles[t][s]=='x')
         {
         loc[0]=0x1F;
         loc[1]=0x1F;
         loc[2]=0x8F;
         }
      else
         loc[0]=loc[1]=loc[2]=0xCA;
      loc+=3;
      }
   }
```

A closer view against a black background is shown below:

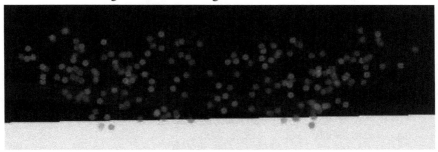

An even closer view shows how the shape is drawn:

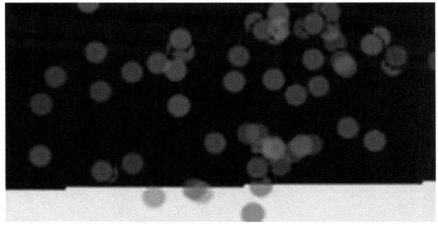

The droplet positions are kept in a list, which is initialized and then updated with each time step (see TIME_DELTA below). The initial positions and velocities are randomized:

```
void makePointList(void)
  {
  float angle,velocity,direction;
  int i;
  motion=1;
  for(i=0;i<numPoints;i++)
    {
    pointList[i][0]=0.0;
    pointList[i][1]=0.0;
    pointList[i][2]=0.0;
    pointTime[i]=0.0;
    angle=(RANDOM_RANGE(60.0,70.0))*M_PI/180.0;
    direction=RANDOM_RANGE(0.0,360.0)*M_PI/180.0;
    pointDirection[i][0]=cos(direction);
    pointDirection[i][1]=sin(direction);
    velocity=MEAN_VELOCITY+RANDOM_RANGE(-0.8,1.);
    pointVelocity[i][0]=velocity*cos(angle);
    pointVelocity[i][1]=velocity*sin(angle);
    colorList[i]=rand()%NUM_COLORS;
    }
  theTime=0.0;
  }
```

The positions are updated based on the velocities and time step and the velocities are diminished by 80% at each step to provide a geometric slowing effect (see *=0.8 below).

```
void updatePointList(void)
  {
  float distance;
  int i;
  motion=0;
  for(i=0;i<numPoints;i++)
    {
    distance=pointVelocity[i][0]*theTime;
    pointList[i][0]=pointDirection[i][0]*distance;
    pointList[i][2]=pointDirection[i][1]*distance;
    pointList[i][1]=(pointVelocity[i][1]
      -0.5*GRAVITY*pointTime[i])*pointTime[i];
    if(pointList[i][1]<=0.0)
      {
      if(distance>EDGE)
        {
        colorList[i]=NUM_COLORS; /* Not moving. */
        continue;
        }
      pointVelocity[i][1]*=0.8;
```

```
        pointTime[i]=0.;
        }
    motion=1;
    pointTime[i]+=TIME_DELTA;
    }
theTime+=TIME_DELTA;
if(!motion&&!spin)
    {
    if(repeat)
      makePointList();
    else
      glutIdleFunc(NULL);
    }
}
```

Chapter 18. Soaring Motion

The skyfly demo included in the OpenGL SDK is truly amazing for its coding simplicity and seeming visual complexity. The scenery (clouds and terrain) are cleverly created and quite compact, based on two bitmaps (clouds.bw and terrain.bw) that are ready for OpenGL.

The spatial variability is more than adequate. This next figure shows an object called a *sprite*:

The programming of this demo is a little different from the previous examples in that the camera moves rather than the objects. There are also *sprites*, which look like paper airplanes and continue to move even after the main scene stops. If you are interested in sprites this is a good example to consider. The paper airplanes are defined as follows:

```
float paper_plane_vertexes[]={
/*Nx    Ny    Nz     Vx     Vy     Vz */
  0.2,  0.0,  0.98,-0.10,  0.00,  0.02,
  0.0,  0.0,  1.00,-0.36,  0.20,-0.04,
  0.0,  0.0,  1.00, 0.36,  0.01,  0.00,
  0.0,  0.0,-1.00,-0.32,  0.02,  0.00,
  0.0,  1.0,  0.00, 0.48,  0.00,-0.06,
  0.0,  1.0,  0.00,-0.30,  0.00,-0.12,
  0.0,-1.0,  0.00, 0.36,-0.01,  0.00,
  0.0,-1.0,  0.00,-0.32,-0.02,  0.00,
  0.0,  0.0,-1.00, 0.36,-0.01,  0.00,
  0.0,  0.0,-1.00,-0.36,-0.20,-0.04,
 -0.2,  0.0,  0.98,-0.10,  0.00,  0.02,
 -0.2,  0.0,-0.98,-0.10,  0.00,  0.02,
  0.0,  0.0,-1.00,-0.36,  0.20,-0.04,
  0.0,  0.0,-1.00, 0.36,  0.01,  0.00,
  0.0,  0.0,  1.00,-0.32,  0.02,  0.00,
  0.0,-1.0,  0.00, 0.48,  0.00,-0.06,
  0.0,-1.0,  0.00,-0.30,  0.00,-0.12,
  0.0,  1.0,  0.00, 0.36,-0.01,  0.00,
  0.0,  1.0,  0.00,-0.32,-0.02,  0.00,
  0.0,  0.0,  1.00, 0.36,-0.01,  0.00,
  0.0,  0.0,  1.00,-0.36,-0.20,-0.04,
  0.2,  0.0,-0.98,-0.10,  0.00,  0.02};
```

The sprites are drawn with the following code:

```
void put_paper_plane(float*source,perfobj_t*pobj)
  {
  int j;
  perfobj_vert_t*pdataptr=(perfobj_vert_t*)pobj->vdata;
  unsigned int*flagsptr=pobj->flags;
  float*sp=source;
  *flagsptr++=PD_DRAW_PAPER_PLANE;
  for(j=0;j<22;j++)
    {
    putn3fdata(sp+0,pdataptr);
    putv3fdata(sp+3,pdataptr);
    sp+=6;
    pdataptr++;
    }
  *flagsptr++=PD_END;
  }

void init_paper_planes(void)
```

```
{
perfobj_t*pobj;
/* create various perf-objs for planes */
pobj=&(SharedData->paper_plane_obj);
pobj->flags=SharedData->paper_plane_flags;
pobj->vdata=(float*)SharedData->paper_plane_verts;
put_paper_plane(paper_plane_vertexes,pobj);
pobj=&(SharedData->paper_plane_start_obj);
pobj->flags=SharedData->paper_plane_start_flags;
*(pobj->flags)=PD_PAPER_PLANE_MODE;
*(pobj->flags+1)=PLANES_START;
*(pobj->flags+2)=PD_END;
pobj=&(SharedData->paper_plane_2ndpass_obj);
pobj->flags=SharedData->paper_plane_2ndpass_flags;
*(pobj->flags)=PD_PAPER_PLANE_MODE;
*(pobj->flags+1)=PLANES_SECOND_PASS;
*(pobj->flags+2)=PD_END;
pobj=&(SharedData->paper_plane_end_obj);
pobj->flags=SharedData->paper_plane_end_flags;
*(pobj->flags)=PD_PAPER_PLANE_MODE;
*(pobj->flags+1)=PLANES_END;
*(pobj->flags+2)=PD_END;
}
```

The soaring sensation is produced by the following section of code:

```
void fly(perfobj_t*viewer_pos)
{
float terrain_z,xpos,ypos,xcntr,ycntr;
float delta_speed=.003;
xcntr=Wxsize/2;
ycntr=Wysize/2;
if(Xgetbutton(RKEY))
  init_positions();
if(Xgetbutton(SPACEKEY))
  Keyboard_mode=!Keyboard_mode;
if(Keyboard_mode)
  {
  /* step-at-a-time debugging mode */
  if(Keyboard_mode && Xgetbutton(LEFTARROWKEY))
    Azimuth-=0.025;
  if(Keyboard_mode && Xgetbutton(RIGHTARROWKEY))
    Azimuth+=0.025;
  if(Keyboard_mode && Xgetbutton(UPARROWKEY))
    {
    X+=cosf(-Azimuth+M_PI/2.)*0.025;
    Y+=sinf(-Azimuth+M_PI/2.)*0.025;
    }
  if(Keyboard_mode && Xgetbutton(DOWNARROWKEY))
    {
    X-=cosf(-Azimuth+M_PI/2.)*0.025;
```

```
      Y-=sinf(-Azimuth+M_PI/2.)*0.025;
      }
    if(Keyboard_mode && Xgetbutton(PAGEUPKEY))
      Z+=0.025;
    if(Keyboard_mode && Xgetbutton(PAGEDOWNKEY))
      Z-=0.025;
    }
  else
    {
    /* simple,mouse-driven flight model */
    if(Xgetbutton(LEFTMOUSE) && Speed<.3)
      Speed+=delta_speed;
    if(Xgetbutton(RIGHTMOUSE) && Speed>-.3)
      Speed-=delta_speed;
    if(Xgetbutton(MIDDLEMOUSE))
      Speed=Speed*.8;
    xpos=(Xgetvaluator(MOUSEX)-xcntr)/
      ((float) Wxsize*14.);
    ypos=(Xgetvaluator(MOUSEY)-ycntr)/
      ((float) Wysize*.5);
    /* move in direction of view */
    Azimuth+=xpos;
    X+=cosf(-Azimuth+M_PI/2.)*Speed;
    Y+=sinf(-Azimuth+M_PI/2.)*Speed;
    Z-=ypos*Speed;
    }
  /* keep from getting too close to terrain */
  terrain_z=terrain_height(X,Y);
  if(Z<terrain_z+.4)
    Z=terrain_z+.4;
  X=max(X,1.);
  X=min(X,GRID_RANGE);
  Y=max(Y,1.);
  Y=min(Y,GRID_RANGE);
  Z=min(Z,20.);
  *((float*) viewer_pos->vdata+0)=X;
  *((float*)viewer_pos->vdata+1)=Y;
  *((float*)viewer_pos->vdata+2)=Z;
  *((float*)viewer_pos->vdata+3)=Azimuth;
  }
```

A deficit method is used to adjust the rate of change of the viewpoint in response to mouse motion. Much of the code is devoted to generating the terrain. While fascinating, this is not the primary concern here, rather motion is our focus. The speed of rendering is a critical aspect of the perceived performance of this demo. Knowing which functions to call and in what order to result in the fastest rendering is critical to achieving this end. With this in mind, consider the following section of code, including comments, which sends a significant portion of the scenery to the rendering engine:

```
/*Notice how the following routines unwind loops and
   pre-compute indexes
 *at compile time. This is crucial in obtaining the
   maximum data transfer
 *from cpu to the graphics pipe.
 */

void drawlitmesh_11(float*op)
  {
  glBegin(GL_TRIANGLE_STRIP);
  /* one */
  glNormal3fv((op+PD_V_NORMAL));
  glVertex3fv((op+PD_V_POINT));
  /* two */
  glNormal3fv((op+(PD_V_SIZE+PD_V_NORMAL)));
  glVertex3fv((op+(PD_V_SIZE+PD_V_POINT)));
  /* three */
  glNormal3fv((op+(2*PD_V_SIZE+PD_V_NORMAL)));
  glVertex3fv((op+(2*PD_V_SIZE+PD_V_POINT)));
  /* four */
  glNormal3fv((op+(3*PD_V_SIZE+PD_V_NORMAL)));
  glVertex3fv((op+(3*PD_V_SIZE+PD_V_POINT)));
  /* five */
  glNormal3fv((op+(4*PD_V_SIZE+PD_V_NORMAL)));
  glVertex3fv((op+(4*PD_V_SIZE+PD_V_POINT)));
  /* six */
  glNormal3fv((op+(5*PD_V_SIZE+PD_V_NORMAL)));
  glVertex3fv((op+(5*PD_V_SIZE+PD_V_POINT)));
  /* seven */
  glNormal3fv((op+(6*PD_V_SIZE+PD_V_NORMAL)));
  glVertex3fv((op+(6*PD_V_SIZE+PD_V_POINT)));
  /* eight */
  glNormal3fv((op+(7*PD_V_SIZE+PD_V_NORMAL)));
  glVertex3fv((op+(7*PD_V_SIZE+PD_V_POINT)));
  /* nine */
  glNormal3fv((op+(8*PD_V_SIZE+PD_V_NORMAL)));
  glVertex3fv((op+(8*PD_V_SIZE+PD_V_POINT)));
  /* ten */
  glNormal3fv((op+(9*PD_V_SIZE+PD_V_NORMAL)));
  glVertex3fv((op+(9*PD_V_SIZE+PD_V_POINT)));
  /* eleven */
  glNormal3fv((op+(10*PD_V_SIZE+PD_V_NORMAL)));
  glVertex3fv((op+(10*PD_V_SIZE+PD_V_POINT)));
  glEnd();
  }
```

Fog adds considerably to the realism. A keystroke (f) is included to toggle the fog on and off. This next view is without fog.

Appendix A. Working with Pixel Contexts

The term *pixel context* is tossed about in OpenGL literature as if it were intuitive or had meaning in a broad context. It doesn't, particularly in the context of Windows programming. The Windows APIs use completely different terminology and the documentation doesn't mention pixel contexts. While the terminology is unfamiliar, the concepts are not.

In order to paint anything in Windows you must have a handle to a *device context*. When this device context is in memory, it's called a *compatible* device context. In order to paint on the display without flicker, you must first build the image in memory and then BitBlt it onto the display. Color images in memory are called DIB sections in Windows. You must select the DIB section into the memory device context. The combination of a memory device context and a DIB section (plus a few other things, including a Z-buffer) is called a pixel context.

OpenGL only works with pixel contexts. You can see what pixel contexts are available by calling DescribePixelFormat(). You select the one you want by calling SetPixelFormat(). You prepare it for use with OpenGL by calling wglCreateContext() and distinguishing this one context from many by calling wglMakeCurrent(). When it comes time to paint it onto the display, you call SwapBuffers(), which just *paints* them rather than actually *swapping* them.

Pixel contexts, along with these virtually undocumented Windows API calls, are defined in wingdi.h and ntgdi.h. Other than facilitating OpenGL rendering, it's not clear why these even exist in the Windows context or why they are linked in gdi32.lib and implemented in gdi32.dll. Whatever the reason, this is what they are and you must utilize them to do anything with OpenGL.

You must first get a pixel context before doing anything with OpenGL. You don't get to *request* (or *specify*) a particular pixel context; rather, you must *select* one from a list that will work for you intend to do. You get a list of available formats by calling DescribePixelFormat(). The following is a typical list of such formats:

index	OpenGL	double buffer	RGBA	need palette	system palette	color bits	depth bits	stencil bits	generic	accele-rated	score	stencil score
1	1	0	1	0	0	32	24	0	0	0	0	0
2	1	0	1	0	0	32	24	0	0	0	0	0
3	1	0	1	0	0	32	24	8	0	1	0	0
4	1	0	1	0	0	32	24	8	0	0	0	0
5	1	0	1	0	0	32	0	0	0	0	0	0
6	1	0	1	0	0	32	0	0	0	0	0	0
7	1	1	1	0	0	32	24	0	0	0	80	0
8	1	1	1	0	0	32	24	0	0	0	80	0
9	1	1	1	0	0	32	24	8	0	1	88	88
10	1	1	1	0	0	32	24	8	0	0	80	80
11	1	1	1	0	0	32	0	0	0	0	64	0
12	1	1	1	0	0	32	0	0	0	0	64	0
13	1	1	1	0	0	32	24	0	0	0	80	0
14	1	1	1	0	0	32	24	0	0	0	80	0
19	0	1	1	0	0	32	24	0	0	0	0	0
90	0	1	1	0	0	32	24	8	0	0	0	0
91	1	0	1	0	0	32	32	8	1	1	0	0
92	1	0	1	0	0	32	16	8	1	0	0	0
93	1	1	1	0	0	32	32	8	1	1	90	90
94	1	1	1	0	0	32	16	8	1	0	82	82
95	1	0	1	0	0	32	32	8	1	1	0	0
96	1	0	1	0	0	32	16	8	1	0	0	0
97	1	1	1	0	0	32	32	8	1	0	82	82
98	1	1	1	0	0	32	16	8	1	0	82	82
99	1	0	0	0	0	32	32	8	1	1	0	0
100	1	0	0	0	0	32	16	8	1	0	0	0
101	1	1	0	0	0	32	32	8	1	1	0	0
102	1	1	0	0	0	32	16	8	1	0	0	0
105	1	0	1	0	0	24	32	8	1	0	0	0
106	1	0	1	0	0	24	16	8	1	0	0	0
107	1	0	0	0	0	24	32	8	1	0	0	0
108	1	0	0	0	0	24	16	8	1	0	0	0
111	1	0	1	0	0	16	32	8	1	0	0	0
112	1	0	1	0	0	16	16	8	1	0	0	0
113	1	0	0	0	0	16	32	8	1	0	0	0
114	1	0	0	0	0	16	16	8	1	0	0	0
125	1	0	0	1	1	4	32	8	1	0	0	0
126	1	0	0	1	1	4	16	8	1	0	0	0

This table has been abbreviated for space, but still illustrates the process you must go through in order to select an appropriate pixel context. First of all, some of the available formats don't even support OpenGL. These are eliminated immediately. Ones that don't support double buffering or require a palette can also be eliminated. OpenGL depends on RGBA, so formats that don't support this can also be eliminated. The color depth should be at least 24 and will paint faster if this matches the depth of the display device context.

The depth bits are used for the Z-buffer and must be at least 16. Generic doesn't matter. Accelerated may draw faster, but is not always available, depending on hardware and drivers. If you want to use stenciling, that can be included in the criteria. I calculate a score for each and pick the one with the highest score. If none of the available formats score above zero, exit the program. The following code snippet implements this selection process:

```
HDC GetBestPixelFormat(HDC hDC,int stencil)
{
int i,j,n,s,sx;
PIXELFORMATDESCRIPTOR pfd;
if((n=DescribePixelFormat(hDC,1,0,NULL))<1)
return(NULL);
j=sx=-1;
for(i=1;i<=n;i++)
{
DescribePixelFormat(hDC,i,
  sizeof(PIXELFORMATDESCRIPTOR),&pfd);
if(!(pfd.dwFlags&PFD_SUPPORT_OPENGL))
 continue;
if(!(pfd.dwFlags&PFD_DOUBLEBUFFER))
 continue;
if(pfd.iPixelType!=PFD_TYPE_RGBA)
 continue;
if(pfd.dwFlags&PFD_NEED_PALETTE)
 continue;
if(pfd.dwFlags&PFD_NEED_SYSTEM_PALETTE)
 continue;
if(pfd.cColorBits<24)
 continue;
if(pfd.cDepthBits<16)
 continue;
if((1<<pfd.cStencilBits)<stencil)
 continue;
s=pfd.cDepthBits/16;
if(pfd.dwFlags&PFD_GENERIC_ACCELERATED)
 s+=2;
if(pfd.cColorBits==GetDeviceCaps(hDC,BITSPIXEL))
 s+=8;
else if(pfd.cColorBits>=24)
 s+=4;
```

```
if(s<sx)
 continue;
sx=s;
j=i;
}
if(j<0)
return(NULL);
DescribePixelFormat(hDC,j,
   sizeof(PIXELFORMATDESCRIPTOR),&pfd);
if(!SetPixelFormat(hDC,j,&pfd))
return(NULL);
return(hDC);
}
```

A pixel context must be selected and implemented. This is a three-step process, as illustrated in the following code snippet:

```
if((pDC=GetBestPixelFormat(hPlot))==0)
   Abort(__LINE__,"can't find best pixel context\nerror
   code %i",GetLastError());
if((rDC=wglCreateContext(pDC))==0)
   Abort(__LINE__,"can't create OpenGL context\nerror
   code %i",GetLastError());
if(!wglMakeCurrent(pDC,rDC))
   Abort(__LINE__,"can't make OpenGL context
   current\nerror code %i",GetLastError());
```

You will also need to declare the following variables:

```
HDC pDC;    /* plot window device context */
HGLRC rDC;  /* OpenGL rendering context */
int pFS;    /* pixel format selector */
PIXELFORMATDESCRIPTOR pFd;
```

The rendering process also has several steps:

```
glClearDepth(1);
glClearColor(0,0,0,0);
glClearStencil(0);
glClear(GL_COLOR_BUFFER_BIT|
   GL_DEPTH_BUFFER_BIT|GL_STENCIL_BUFFER_BIT);
insert rendering instructions here
guFinish();
SwapBuffers(pDC);
```

Appendix B. Working with Textures

Textures are 32-bit (DWORD) bitmaps ordered: RGBA. These don't have a header, as is the case with a Windows BITMAP (i.e., BITMAPINFOHEADER structure). Instead, the dimensions are specified in a call to the rendering engine:

```
glTexImage2D(GL_TEXTURE_2D,0,3,bi->biWidth,
    bi->biHeight,0,GL_BGR_EXT,
    GL_UNSIGNED_BYTE,(BYTE*)bits);
```

The RGBA bits are entered by row and in the same order (bottom up) as a Windows BITMAP. The width and height must both be a power of two, though not necessarily the same (i.e., 2, 4, 8, 16, 32, 64, 128, 256, 512, or 1024). Texture bitmaps can be quite large, considering there is no compression. Neither Windows nor OpenGL recognize JPEGs as such. If you want to keep the texture as a JPEG, you must also provide your own code to unpack it. Such a code (jpeg6b.c) can be found in the online archive accompanying this and several other of my texts. The JPEGS can easily be handled as resources and loaded when a program starts up. The following is a typical section of a resource file (*.RC):

```
#undef RT_RCDATA
#define RT_RCDATA 0xA

Agate           RT_RCDATA  "agate.jpg"
BlackGranite    RT_RCDATA  "blackgranite.jpg"
Lapis           RT_RCDATA  "lapis.jpg"
Malachite       RT_RCDATA  "malachite.jpg"
Marble          RT_RCDATA  "marble.jpg"
Oak             RT_RCDATA  "oak.jpg"
Pedauk          RT_RCDATA  "pedauk.jpg"
Purpleheart     RT_RCDATA  "purpleheart.jpg"
Walnut          RT_RCDATA  "walnut.jpg"
WhiteGranite    RT_RCDATA  "whitegranite.jpg"
Yew             RT_RCDATA  "yew.jpg"
Kewazinga       RT_RCDATA  "kewazinga.jpg"
```

Note the redefinition of constant **RT_RCDATA**, which is used for user-defined unstructured binary objects. Some versions of Visual Studio contain a bug. If you don't redefine this constant in the resource file, you will not be able later to load the resource. The other types (e.g., ICON, BITMAP, DIALOG) appear to work well enough. It is also not necessary to redefine RT_RCDATA in the source code (*.C). Preparation of 24-bit images is a simple reordering (don't forget that Windows bitmaps are aligned on DWORD boundaries, while OpenGL bitmaps aren't).

```
wide=4*((bm->biWidth*24+31)/32);
add=wide-3*bm->biWidth;
for(h=0;h<bm->biHeight;h++)
    {
```

89

```
for(w=0;w<bm->biWidth;w++)
  {
  r=*bits++;
  g=*bits++;
  b=*bits++;
  *stib++=b;
  *stib++=g;
  *stib++=r;
  }
bits+=add;
}
```

Preparation of palette-based (8 bit or less) bitmaps is straightforward:

```
if(bHead->biBitCount<=8)
  {
  map=allocate(__LINE__,bHead->biWidth*bHead-
  >biHeight*3,1);
  pal=((BYTE*)bHead)+sizeof(BITMAPINFOHEADER);
  pix=pal+bHead->biClrUsed*sizeof(DWORD);
  if(bHead->biBitCount==8)
    {
    for(h=i=j=0;h<bHead->biHeight;h++)
      {
      for(w=0;w<bHead->biWidth;w++)
        {
        k=pix[i++];
        map[j++]=pal[4*k];
        map[j++]=pal[4*k+1];
        map[j++]=pal[4*k+2];
        }
      }
    }
```

Appendix C. Working with Resources

Windows resource objects can be anything from lists (including meshes) to bitmaps to surfaces (such as topography). These are defined in the resource file (*.RC), compiled with the resource compiler (to produce a file named *.res), and embedded in the executable (*.exe) by the linker. Like object modules (*.obj) these can be deleted once the executable has been created, as they serve no further purpose (see the several batch files _compile.bat in the online archive). Each resource has a type (ICON, BITMAP, DIALOG, or user-defined: RT_RCDATA). Loading a resource is a four-step process:

1) Find the resource (locates the resource)

2) Load the resource (doesn't actually load the resource)

3) Lock the resource (actually loads the resource)

4) Get the resource size (tells you how big it is)

This is illustrated by the following code snippet:

```
typedef struct{DWORD size;void*data;}RESOURCE;
RESOURCE LoadTexture(char*type,char*rname)
  {
  HGLOBAL rLoad;
  HRSRC rFind;
  static RESOURCE res;
  if((rFind=FindResource(hInst,rname,RT_RCDATA))==NULL)
    Abort(__LINE__,"can't find resource %s\nWindows
    error code %li",rname,GetLastError());
  if((rLoad=LoadResource(hInst,rFind))==NULL)
    Abort(__LINE__,"can't load resource %s\nWindows
    error code %li",rname,GetLastError());
  if((res.data=LockResource(rLoad))==NULL)
    Abort(__LINE__,"can't lock resource %s\nWindows
    error code %li",rname,GetLastError());
  res.size=SizeofResource(hInst,rFind));
  return(res);
  }
```

As the RESOURCE structure is larger than the EAX register on an Intel processor, you must make the variable res static; otherwise, returning will generate a stack overflow (a fatal protection fault). The JPEG format is very efficient for storing images and saves a lot of space. These are very convenient and easy to unpack after loading (see jpeg6b.c in the online archive). The GIF format is also compact and easy to implement (see gif89a.c in the online archive). There are many other compression algorithms, which could be used to reduce the size of other data structures. I often use Lempel-Ziv/Arithmetic compression for this task.

You could load a bitmap resource directly using the API call LoadBitmap(); however, this returns a handle to the bitmap and not the bitmap itself. From the

91

handle, you would need to follow this up with a call to GetObject() in order to get a pointer to the actual bitmap, which is actually a DIBSECTION (device independent bitmap). If you store a BMP file as a binary resource the file header will be at the front of the data block, so you must skip over this in order to get a pointer to the bitmap itself, as illustrated in the following code snippet:

```
BITMAPINFOHEADER*LoadBMP(char*name)
  {
  return((BITMAPINFOHEADER*)(((BYTE*)GetResource(
    hInst,name,RT_RCDATA))+sizeof(BITMAPFILEHEADER)));
  }
```

You first hard type the pointer to a BYTE* then add the size of the file header (14 bytes) then hard type the result to the desired pointer. This presumes that you stored the bitmap in the resource file as:

```
name RT_RCDATA "image.bmp"
```

Appendix D. Working with Lists

In Chapter 8 we saw that a *list* could be used to streamline definition and rendering of a sphere with a texture. This is a very simple list and is created with three steps:

1) Get an assigned integer

2) Fill the list

3) Close the list

For the Earth example, this becomes:

```
gEarth=glGenLists(1);
glNewList(gEarth,GL_COMPILE);
gluSphere(Quadric,2.,24,24);
glEndList();
```

Lists can be quite useful. While they don't necessarily speed up rendering, they can simplify implementation, at least from code appearance. One example would be to define each of the chess pieces as a list if polygons. You could then refer to each one in the rendering process by the single integer assigned by OpenGL by calling glGenLists(). The Olympic ring demo, gear demo, blue pony, and dino examples use this method. Several of the teapot examples also build a list.

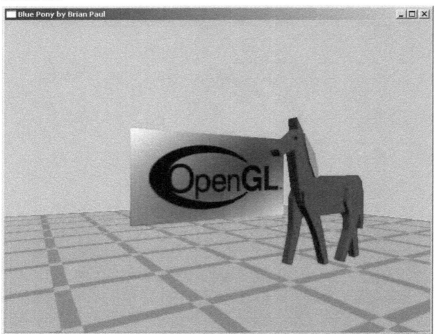

The list used in the blue pony demo (written by Brian Paul) is shown below:

```
void MakePony(void)
  {
  Pony=glGenLists(1);
  glNewList(Pony,GL_COMPILE);
  glMaterialfv(GL_FRONT,GL_AMBIENT_AND_DIFFUSE,blue);
  ExtrudePart(sizeof(PonyVerts)/sizeof(GLfloat)/2,
    PonyVerts,PonyDepth);
  glMaterialfv(GL_FRONT,GL_AMBIENT_AND_DIFFUSE,black);
  glNormal3f(0.0,0.0,1.0);
  glBegin(GL_POLYGON);
  glVertex3f(EyePos[0]-EyeSize,EyePos[1]-EyeSize,
    EyePos[2]);
  glVertex3f(EyePos[0]+EyeSize,EyePos[1]-EyeSize,
    EyePos[2]);
  glVertex3f(EyePos[0]+EyeSize,EyePos[1]+EyeSize,
    EyePos[2]);
  glVertex3f(EyePos[0]-EyeSize,EyePos[1]+EyeSize,
    EyePos[2]);
  glEnd();
  glNormal3f(0.0,0.0,-1.0);
  glBegin(GL_POLYGON);
  glVertex3f(EyePos[0]-EyeSize,EyePos[1]+EyeSize,
    -EyePos[2]);
  glVertex3f(EyePos[0]+EyeSize,EyePos[1]+EyeSize,
    -EyePos[2]);
  glVertex3f(EyePos[C]+EyeSize,EyePos[1]-EyeSize,
    -EyePos[2]);
  glVertex3f(EyePos[0]-EyeSize,EyePos[1]-EyeSize,
    -EyePos[2]);
  glEnd();
  glEndList();
  Mane=glGenLists(1);
  glNewList(Mane,GL_COMPILE);
  glMaterialfv(GL_FRONT,GL_AMBIENT_AND_DIFFUSE,
    pink);
  ExtrudePart(sizeof(ManeVerts)/sizeof(GLfloat)/2,
    ManeVerts,ManeDepth);
  glEndList();
  FrontLeg=glGenLists(1);
  glNewList(FrontLeg,GL_COMPILE);
  glMaterialfv(GL_FRONT,GL_AMBIENT_AND_DIFFUSE,
    blue);
  ExtrudePart(sizecf(FrontLegVerts)/sizeof(GLfloat)/2,
    FrontLegVerts,LegDepth);
  glEndList();
  BackLeg=glGenLists(1);
  glNewList(BackLeg,GL_COMPILE);
  glMaterialfv(GL_FRONT,GL_AMBIENT_AND_DIFFUSE,blue);
```

```
ExtrudePart(sizeof(BackLegVerts)/sizeof(GLfloat)/2,
  BackLegVerts,LegDepth);
glEndList();
}
```

In order to facilitate motion, the pony is broken into four pieces: pony, mane, front leg, and back leg, using four calls to glGenLists(). Each list is a combination of several polygons, defined in data statements elsewhere in the code. The colors (blue, black, and pink) are also defined elsewhere in data statements. The Olympic ring, dino, gear, and blue pony demos (along with many others) can be found in the online archive accompanying *3D Rendering in Windows*. The gears in that demo are implemented as lists. Consider the following code:

```
/* make the gears */
gear1=glGenLists(1);
glNewList(gear1,GL_COMPILE);
glMaterialfv(GL_FRONT,GL_AMBIENT_AND_DIFFUSE,red);
gear(1.0,4.0,1.0,20,0.7);
glEndList();
gear2=glGenLists(1);
glNewList(gear2,GL_COMPILE);
glMaterialfv(GL_FRONT,GL_AMBIENT_AND_DIFFUSE,green);
gear(0.5,2.0,2.0,10,0.7);
glEndList();
gear3=glGenLists(1);
glNewList(gear3,GL_COMPILE);
glMaterialfv(GL_FRONT,GL_AMBIENT_AND_DIFFUSE,blue);
gear(1.3,2.0,0.5,10,0.7);
glEndList();
```

and then drawn referencing the respective lists:

```
glPushMatrix();
glTranslatef(-3.0,-2.0,0.0);
glRotatef(angle,0.0,0.0,1.0);
glCallList(gear1);
glPopMatrix();
glPushMatrix();
glTranslatef(3.1,-2.0,0.0);
glRotatef(-2.0*angle-9.0,0.0,0.0,1.0);
glCallList(gear2);
glPopMatrix();
glPushMatrix();
glTranslatef(-3.1,4.2,0.0);
glRotatef(-2.0*angle-25.0,0.0,0.0,1.0);
glCallList(gear3);
glPopMatrix();
glPopMatrix();
glutSwapBuffers();
```

The dinosaur is also defined and then rendered as a list:

Appendix E. Working with Collections

A mesh is a user-defined collection of polygons having the same shape, most often triangles. These are defined by a structure:

```
typedef struct{float x1,x2,x3,y1,y2,y3,z1,z2,z3;DWORD
    color;}MESH;
```

It is most convenient to define a terminating characteristic rather than keep track of a count for each mesh. Meshes may be terminated by an obvious outlying value, such as FLT_MAX, or by an impossible color, such as −1 (which is 0xFFFFFFFF). As colors span RGB, only the first 24 bits on an Intel processor (Big Endian) are used, namely 0x00FFFFFF. If there is any non-zero value in the high byte, this flags the end of the mesh.

```
if((color&0xFF000000)!=0)
```

A section of the fire extinguisher mesh from Chapter 3 is listed below:

```
MESH FireExtinguisher[]={
{ 0.07F,0.75F, 0.00F, 0.01F,0.73F, 0.06F, 0.04F,0.73F,
    0.08F,red},
{ 0.07F,0.75F, 0.00F,-0.01F,0.73F,-0.03F,-0.02F,0.73F,
    0.00F,red},
{ 0.07F,0.75F, 0.00F,-0.02F,0.73F, 0.00F,-0.01F,0.73F,
    0.03F,red},
etc.
{-0.03F,0.71F, 0.07F, 0.03F,0.71F, 0.11F, 0.03F,0.82F,
    0.11F,black},
{-0.02F,0.71F,-0.07F,-0.05F,0.82F, 0.00F,-0.02F,0.82F,-
    0.07F,black},
{-0.13F,1.00F,-0.01F,-0.17F,0.97F,-0.02F,-0.18F,0.99F,-
    0.01F,black},
etc.
{ 0.00F,0.00F, 0.00F, 0.00F,0.00F, 0.00F, 0.00F,0.00F,
    0.00F,-1}};
```

Many of the objects in the demos found in the online archive are meshes. As you look through the examples, you will find most of these in files like: name.h. These are included by the compiler and become static data statements that are placed accordingly in the executable image and readily accessed by the code, often without requiring any additional processing, other than being passed to the rendering engine.

It is customary for these to be centered about (0,0,0) and oriented toward the viewer. When drawing the scene, precede the mesh with the desired displacement glTranslatef() and rotation glRotatef(). In most cases the translation will precede the rotation, but not always, depending on the desired effect. Controlling the order of these two calls can add considerable complexity to your scene with very little coding effort.

The forklift used in the MSRE example is a single mesh, which is rendered as shown below:

Appendix F. Working with Topography

The Sandy Run model is all about topography. It was created to simulate and visualize an actual flooding event that resulted from a minivan being washed down an embankment during a torrential rain. The minivan was temporarily stuck under a railroad trestle, backing water up into the adjacent downtown area long enough to fill the basement of two buildings and cause considerable damage. The part played by the minivan wasn't discovered right away because a tow truck had removed it and some time elapsed between before anyone realized that it had been parked upstream of the trestle and was removed from the downstream area. Matching paint scrapings along the walls of the trestle confirmed this was the cause of the temporary flooding.

The Sandy Run demo is based on actual topography. The ETTP and Manhattan Project Museum demo also contain actual topography. This information was supplied in the form of contours. The surface was created by triangularization (i.e., 2D meshing) of the contours.

A closer view of the mesh is shown in this next figure:

Flooding is accomplished by drawing a blue flood plane and allowing it to intersect with the 3D surface of the topography. The water surface was calibrated based on measurements and observations, including eyewitness accounts of when the water reached specific locations. The aerial view is painted on top of the topography as a texture.

The surface is simply a collection of 3D triangles. The XZ locations are provided by the mesh generator and the Y location of the points comes from the contour values. The ETTP topography triangles and building outlines (hexahedra) are shown in this next figure:

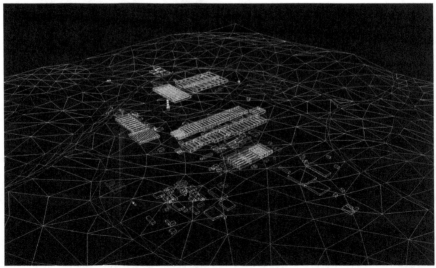

also by D. James Benton

3D Articulation: Using OpenGL, ISBN-9798596362480, Amazon, 2021 (book 3 in the 3D series).

3D Rendering in Windows: How to display three-dimensional objects in Windows with and without OpenGL, ISBN-9781520339610, Amazon, 2016 (book 1 in the 3D series).

A Synergy of Short Stories: The whole may be greater than the sum of the parts, ISBN-9781520340319, Amazon, 2016.

Azeotropes: Behavior and Application, ISBN-9798609748997, Amazon, 2020.

bat-Elohim: Book 3 in the Little Star Trilogy, ISBN-9781686148682, Amazon, 2019.

Boilers: Performance and Testing, ISBN: 9798789062517, Amazon 2021.

Combined 3D Rendering Series: 3D Rendering in Windows®, 3D Models in Motion, and 3D Articulation, ISBN-9798484417032, Amazon, 2021.

Complex Variables: Practical Applications, ISBN-9781794250437, Amazon, 2019.

Compression & Encryption: Algorithms & Software, ISBN-9781081008826, Amazon, 2019.

Computational Fluid Dynamics: an Overview of Methods, ISBN-9781672393775, Amazon, 2019.

Computer Simulation of Power Systems: Programming Strategies and Practical Examples, ISBN-9781696218184, Amazon, 2019.

Contaminant Transport: A Numerical Approach, ISBN-9798461733216, Amazon, 2021.

CPUnleashed! Tapping Processor Speed, ISBN-9798421420361, Amazon, 2022.

Curve-Fitting: The Science and Art of Approximation, ISBN-9781520339542, Amazon, 2016.

Death by Tie: It was the best of ties. It was the worst of ties. It's what got him killed., ISBN-9798398745931, Amazon, 2023.

Differential Equations: Numerical Methods for Solving, ISBN-9781983004162, Amazon, 2018.

Equations of State: A Graphical Comparison, ISBN-9798843139520, Amazon, 2022.

Evaporative Cooling: The Science of Beating the Heat, ISBN-9781520913346, Amazon, 2017.

Forecasting: Extrapolation and Projection, ISBN-9798394019494, Amazon 2023.

Heat Engines: Thermodynamics, Cycles, & Performance Curves, ISBN-9798486886836, Amazon, 2021.

Heat Exchangers: Performance Prediction & Evaluation, ISBN-9781973589327, Amazon, 2017.

Heat Recovery Steam Generators: Thermal Design and Testing, ISBN-9781691029365, Amazon, 2019.

Heat Transfer: Heat Exchangers, Heat Recovery Steam Generators, & Cooling Towers, ISBN-9798487417831, Amazon, 2021.

Heat Transfer Examples: Practical Problems Solved, ISBN-9798390610763, Amazon, 2023.

The Kick-Start Murders: Visualize revenge, ISBN-9798759083375, Amazon, 2021.

Jamie2: Innocence is easily lost and cannot be restored, ISBN-9781520339375, Amazon, 2016-18.

Kyle Cooper Mysteries: Kick Start, Monte Carlo, and Waterfront Murders, ISBN-9798829365943, Amazon, 2022.

The Last Seraph: Sequel to Little Star, ISBN-9781726802253, Amazon, 2018.

Little Star: God doesn't do things the way we expect Him to. He's better than that! ISBN-9781520338903, Amazon, 2015-17.

Living Math: Seeing mathematics in every day life (and appreciating it more too), ISBN-9781520336992, Amazon, 2016.

Lost Cause: If only history could be changed..., ISBN-9781521173770, Amazon, 2017.

Mass Transfer: Diffusion & Convection, ISBN-9798702403106, Amazon, 2021.

Mill Town Destiny: The Hand of Providence brought them together to rescue the mill, the town, and each other, ISBN-9781520864679, Amazon, 2017.

Monte Carlo Murders: Who Killed Who and Why, ISBN-9798829341848, Amazon, 2022.

Monte Carlo Simulation: The Art of Random Process Characterization, ISBN-9781980577874, Amazon, 2018.

Nonlinear Equations: Numerical Methods for Solving, ISBN-9781717767318, Amazon, 2018.

Numerical Calculus: Differentiation and Integration, ISBN-9781980680901, Amazon, 2018.

Numerical Methods: Nonlinear Equations, Numerical Calculus, & Differential Equations, ISBN-9798486246845, Amazon, 2021.

Orthogonal Functions: The Many Uses of, ISBN-9781719876162, Amazon, 2018.

Overwhelming Evidence: A Pilgrimage, ISBN-9798515642211, Amazon, 2021.

Particle Tracking: Computational Strategies and Diverse Examples, ISBN-9781692512651, Amazon, 2019.

Plumes: Delineation & Transport, ISBN-9781702292771, Amazon, 2019.

Power Plant Performance Curves: for Testing and Dispatch, ISBN-9798640192698, Amazon, 2020.

Practical Linear Algebra: Principles & Software, ISBN-9798860910584, Amazon, 2023.

Props, Fans, & Pumps: Design & Performance, ISBN-9798645391195, Amazon, 2020.

Remediation: Contaminant Transport, Particle Tracking, & Plumes, ISBN-9798485651190, Amazon, 2021.

ROFL: Rolling on the Floor Laughing, ISBN-9781973300007, Amazon, 2017.

Seminole Rain: You don't choose destiny. It chooses you, ISBN-9798668502196, Amazon, 2020.

Septillionth: 1 in 10^{24}, ISBN-9798410762472, Amazon, 2022.

Software Development: Targeted Applications, ISBN-9798850653989, Amazon, 2023.

Software Recipes: Proven Tools, ISBN-9798815229556, Amazon, 2022.

Steam 2020: to 150 GPa and 6000 K, ISBN-9798634643830, Amazon, 2020.

Thermochemical Reactions: Numerical Solutions, ISBN-9781073417872, Amazon, 2019.

Thermodynamic and Transport Properties of Fluids, ISBN-9781092120845, Amazon, 2019.

Thermodynamic Cycles: Effective Modeling Strategies for Software Development, ISBN-9781070934372, Amazon, 2019.

Thermodynamics - Theory & Practice: The science of energy and power, ISBN-9781520339795, Amazon, 2016.

Version-Independent Programming: Code Development Guidelines for the Windows® Operating System, ISBN-9781520339146, Amazon, 2016.

The Waterfront Murders: As you sow, so shall you reap, ISBN-9798611314500, Amazon, 2020.

Weather Data: Where To Get It and How To Process It, ISBN-9798868037894, Amazon, 2023.